D1551711

At Issue

Beauty Pageants

Other Books in the At Issue Series:

At Issue

Beauty Pageants

Noël Merino, Book Editor

GREENHAVEN PRESS
A part of Gale, Cengage Learning

GALE
CENGAGE Learning

Detroit • New York • San Francisco • New Haven, Conn • Waterville, Maine • London

Christine Nasso, *Publisher*
Elizabeth Des Chenes, *Managing Editor*

© 2010 Greenhaven Press, a part of Gale, Cengage Learning.

Gale and Greenhaven Press are registered trademarks used herein under license.

For more information, contact:
Greenhaven Press
27500 Drake Rd.
Farmington Hills, MI 48331-3535
Or you can visit our Internet site at gale.cengage.com

For product information and technology assistance, contact us at

Gale Customer Support, 1-800-877-4253
For permission to use material from this text or product, submit all requests online at
www.cengage.com/permissions

Further permissions questions can be emailed to permissionrequest@cengage.com

Articles in Greenhaven Press anthologies are often edited for length to meet page requirements. In addition, original titles of these works are changed to clearly present the main thesis and to explicitly indicate the author's opinion. Every effort is made to ensure that Greenhaven Press accurately reflects the original intent of the authors. Every effort has been made to trace the owners of copyrighted material.

Cover image © Images.com/Corbis.

LIBRARY OF CONGRESS CATALOGING-IN-PUBLICATION DATA

Beauty pageants / Noël Merino, book editor.
    p. cm. -- (At issue)
Includes bibliographical references and index.
ISBN 978-0-7377-4536-8 (hardcover)
ISBN 978-0-7377-4537-5 (pbk.)
1. Beauty contests--Juvenile literature. I. Merino, Noël
    HQ1219.B349 2009
    305.4--dc22

                                        2009022928

Printed in the United States of America
2 3 4 5 6 7 13 12 11 10 09

Contents

Introduction

The debate about beauty pageants—covering such topics as feminism, exploitation, and self esteem—is as varied as the kind of beauty pageants now in existence. While beauty pageants range from the traditional competitions for single women in their late teens or early twenties, to pageants for children, to even one for women who have lost limbs to landmines, they all share one common element: beauty is a major factor in determining the outcome.

Perhaps the most well-known beauty pageant in the United States is the Miss America pageant, a contest for unmarried, childless women between the ages of seventeen and twenty-four, with competitions held at the local, state, and national levels. First held in Atlantic City in 1921 as solely a beauty contest, the Miss America Organization currently emphasizes the scholarship-granting component of its pageant, offering over $40 million in cash and tuition scholarship assistance each year. The Miss America competition does include a talent portion and an interview, but it also includes portions where the contestants compete in eveningwear and in swimsuits.

Among other well-known pageants is the Miss USA pageant, the winner of which goes on to compete in the Miss Universe pageant. The Miss Universe pageant program, in operation since 1952, differs from the Miss America pageant in that there are no scholarships given and there is no talent portion of the competition. Women in the Miss USA pageant must be between eighteen and twenty-seven years old, and must never have been married or have given birth. The Miss Teen USA pageant, also put on by the Miss Universe Organization, allows young, single, childless women between fifteen and nineteen to compete.

Other worldwide pageants that are similar to Miss Universe include the Miss World pageant, based in the United

Kingdom; the Miss Earth pageant, which focuses on raising environmental awareness; and the Miss Tourism Queen International pageant, which is based in China and focuses on enhancing tourism in the countries of the contestants. In addition, there are a variety of similar pageants for young women all over the world that focus on beauty as a core component of the competition.

A variety of other beauty pageants have emerged that either do not have the stringent entry requirements as the more popular pageants, or that have different standards of beauty than the most popular pageants. For example, the Mrs. America and Mrs. World pageants are for married women who may or may not have children. The Ms. Classic Beauty pageant caters to full-figured women who wear a size ten or larger, has no age or marital requirement, and only has 10 percent of the score contingent on looks. The Mr. World pageant is a beauty pageant for men. The Miss Landmine pageant involves a competition among women, of varied age and marital status, who have been injured by landmines. The Ms. Wheelchair America pageant involves female participants of any marital status who use a wheelchair for daily mobility.

In addition to the Miss Teen USA pageant, there are a variety of pageants that cater to young contestants. The Universal Royalty Pageant holds competitions for different age groups dozens of times during the year, and children can participate as soon as they are able to sit up on their own. There are a variety of contests to enter, with the majority of them revolving around the looks of the child contestants.

Beauty pageants for young women have been criticized by feminists because of the perception that they objectify women, emphasizing their physical appearance over all else. But those in favor of the pageants argue that there is no shame in showing off one's beauty, fitness, and health. Beauty pageants involving those who are injured by landmines or in wheelchairs are considered exploitative by some, whereas others consider them liberating for the disabled and important for expanding our conceptions of beauty. Pageants involving children have opponents who charge that the contests sexualize children, while proponents of the contests claim that the pageants are a learning opportunity and a confidence booster for children. Despite the outcry over beauty pageants, many remain popular as forms of entertainment. The disagreements about the harms and benefits of beauty pageants are a few of the topics covered in the viewpoints included in *At Issue: Beauty Pageants.*

The Cultural Relevance of Beauty Pageants Is Waning

Hilary Levey

Hilary Levey is a graduate student in sociology at Princeton University.

Women who compete in beauty pageants, such as Miss America, have often been a part of the beauty pageant world from a young age. As the popularity of child beauty pageants grows, society's interest in adult women beauty pageants is diminishing. The popularity of beauty pageants has waxed and waned since their inception over a century ago. The cultural relevance of beauty pageants in the twenty-first century, with the advent of a variety of reality shows involving winners and losers, is diminishing even as the pageants maintain a loyal base of fervent admirers.

"I've heard you have a better chance of having a son in the Superbowl than you do a daughter in the Miss America Pageant."

So said one of the crowned women standing around and gossiping with similarly clad queens in crowns and short-shorts with sashes draped across their chests proclaiming their representative states. Cameras caught their every facial expression, part of the first-ever Pageant School for the Miss America Pageant, a two-hour special that aired on Country Music Television (CMT) prior to the Pageant on January 29, 2007, showing the 52 contestants meeting in Los Angeles to prepare for the national event.

A camera zoomed in on one of the other women as her heavily painted lips fell open, exclaiming, "How in the heck did I get here? Those odds are ah-mazing!" Next to her, Miss Alabama, an elder stateswoman of the group, nodded and sagely commented, "There are so many girls who want to be here. We're the lucky ones."

Miss Alabama 2006, Melinda Toole, who competed in 23 preliminary pageants just to get a chance to compete in her state pageant—let alone at the "big show," or the national Miss America event—should know, as she is what is known as a "Pageant Patty." Pageant Patties are the stereotypical beauty pageant contestants who want world peace, never have a hair out of place in their hair-spray-shellacked, football-helmet hair-dos, and wear gowns that look like something out of *Dallas*. Such women take the world of pageantry seriously. They may have known the glitz and glamour of this life since before they could walk, carried onto stages in hotel ballrooms by their moms to prepare them to pursue the crown that famously represents "the dreams of a million girls who are more than pretty."

Even as the number of child pageants grows ... the grandest pageant of all, the Miss America Pageant, has struggled.

Little Miss Sunshine savaged this child beauty-pageant circuit in 2006. At the beginning of the movie, little Olive Hoover shrieks in delight when she hears a phone message telling her that she is eligible to compete in the Little Miss Sunshine Pageant. The girl who was crowned at the qualifying pageant got sick, so Olive, as runner-up, advanced to the next stage of competition. In reaction Olive ran around the house shouting, "I won! I won! I won!" unconcerned that she actually had not.

The majority of child pageants do not follow the elimination-style format used in *Little Miss Sunshine*. Instead, if you can pay the big entry fees, you are welcome to represent any city or state in the hopes of being named America's Gorgeous Girl (for $325) or the Ultimate Supreme at Southern Sparkles & Smilz ($425). But since most of us are familiar with this Miss America format—based on local preliminaries, state competitions, and then a national contest—it made sense for Olive to be subject to the tried-and-true pageant formula. (This elimination system was also used in pageant films like *Miss Congeniality* [2000], *Drop Dead Gorgeous* [1999], and *Beautiful* [2000].)

Even as the number of child pageants grows, and attention to child and adult pageants in the media increases both in movie theaters and on reality television series like Bravo's 2005 *Showbiz Moms & Dads* and MTV's 2006–7 *Tiara Girls*, the grandest pageant of all, the Miss America Pageant, has struggled. 2006 was the first year it was held outside of Atlantic City (in Las Vegas). It was also the first time since 1954 that network TV did not carry the Pageant (it was on the cable channel CMT). Finally, it took place for the first time in January and on a Monday night instead of Saturday (the second Saturday after Labor Day had been tradition since 1921). These changes were due to dwindling ratings and the subsequent loss of network sponsorship.

The 2007 Pageant added another twist, as Miss America went the way of reality TV with its Pageant School. Promoters like to say they are "going Hollywood" and "changing with the times," but 2007 witnessed the lowest ratings ever for the live broadcast. While it remains the largest source of scholarship money for women in the world, albeit with smaller awards due to the loss of network support, the Pageant (with a capital P, as it is known to insiders) continues its slow decline.

Though Miss America is considered "the grandmother" of all pageants, it was not the first beauty pageant held in the United States. That distinction goes to an event called Miss United States that took place in Reheboth Beach, Delaware, in 1880, featuring women in their bathing suits. After this, pageants began springing up at carnivals and fairs and on beaches along both coasts, available for every age and body type.

In 1921 a group of Atlantic City businessmen came up with the idea of adding a beauty contest to the fall festival they had started the year before. They were hoping to keep visitors on the shore after Labor Day, the traditional end of the summer season, and adding a pageant was another way to bring in revenue. They held the first contest, called The Most Beautiful Bathing Girl in America, on September 6, 1921, with only seven bathing-suit-clad beauties. By the next year there were 57 contestants. The contest struck a cultural nerve and continued to grow in popularity throughout the Roaring '20s, informally renamed the Miss America Pageant.

Though Miss America is considered "the grandmother" of all pageants, it was not the first beauty pageant held in the United States.

Despite its popularity, the early Pageant received some unfavorable reviews, the result of uncertainty and tensions over changes in women's place in society. The year before the Pageant's inception, in 1920, women had received the right to vote. The suffragist movement had been one of the first social movements organized by and for women, and many in society, especially men, saw these female leaders as violating traditional gender roles. Critics also did not approve when suffragists used public pageantry and their bodies to attract attention: wearing sashes and banners to public protests was seen as too forward and not "proper" for a lady (interestingly, those sashes are the source of the sashes that pageant queens wear today).

By 1928 the Pageant succumbed to public negativity and was discontinued. With the onset of the Great Depression, the event continued to languish. It was resurrected in 1933 in an effort to increase tourism in Atlantic City, but was again shelved in 1934.

Everything changed in 1935, when Lenora Slaughter from St. Petersburg, Florida, traveled up North to take over, making the Pageant what it is today. As Bess Myerson, Miss America 1945, said of Slaughter, "She picked up the pageant by its bathing suit straps and put it in an evening gown." In 1938 Slaughter made the talent portion of the competition mandatory; in 1941 she changed the name to The Miss America Pageant, and in 1945 she gave out the first scholarship to the winner. She devised a chaperone system by which female volunteers from Atlantic City kept the contestants away from men during the competition, including their fathers. All of Slaughter's efforts were a calculated attempt to attract "ladies" to the Pageant.

Slaughter's reign continued as the Pageant was first televised in 1954, ushering in its golden era. At its height in 1961, the Pageant commanded a whopping 75 percent share of the television audience. It remains the longest-running television show, though with much lower ratings today.

Even though the Pageant had been criticized as being too revealing for women, by the 1960s it was being called prudish, as women began wearing bikinis instead of modest one-piece suits. The Women's Liberation Movement, which had been trying to gain national attention for some time, hit the jackpot on September 7, 1968, with its Miss America protest. About 100 women gathered on the New Jersey boardwalk and staged their own "pageant." They threw symbols of "female oppression" into a trashcan, including their bras; but they did not actually burn them, despite the famous moniker, since they could not get the necessary permit. Scholar Susan J. Douglas argues that social historians have underestimated the importance of this protest, since it almost single-handedly gave the women's movement a national audience. She describes the scene, saying, "They seemed to take a cheerful delight in trashing one of the country's most sacred and closely followed rituals, the only TV show, claimed Richard Nixon, that he let Tricia and Julie stay up late to watch."

The Pageant buzzed along through the 1970s, facing declining ratings, but still qualifying as one of the Top 10 rated shows every year. Then came scandals in the 1980s, starting with the dismissal of the legendary emcee Bert Parks. The biggest scandal occurred in 1984 when Vanessa Williams, the first African-American Miss America, also became the first woman to give up her title after nude photos of her with a woman appeared in *Penthouse* (still the best-selling issue).

Yet the Pageant endured, despite flagging ratings. As William Goldman wrote in his 1990 exposé on being a Pageant judge, "Lately it's been drifting. Lots of reasons: feminism, a proliferation of clone contests, a sense that there was something 19th-century about the endeavor.... [But] it was still the dream of thousands of young women all across the country (but mainly in small towns). It was still a famous name."

Even though the Pageant had been criticized as being too revealing for women, by the 1960s it was being called prudish.

But how can the Miss America Pageant retain any cultural relevance today when it must contend not only with feminism but with reality TV shows where Americans get to choose the winners? What does it mean that three of the biggest names from *American Idol*—Tamyra Gray, Diana DeGarmo, and Carrie Underwood—competed in Miss America pageants but never made it very far in the system? In 2006 I traveled to Las Vegas to see how the Pageant was "changing with the times." It was the first time I had been to the Pageant since 1990, when

I went to Atlantic City with my mother, herself a former Miss America (Michigan, 1970). Because I was 25, it was the last year that I was eligible to be a contestant in the Pageant. While I had never wanted to be Miss America, it suddenly annoyed me to know that this ship had sailed.

The dream was still alive for the hundreds of girls who attended the 2006 Pageant. As I sat in the theater at the Aladdin Hotel on the Strip, I was enclosed in a sea of crowns. Little girls and teenagers attended the Pageant in droves, many wearing the crowns and sashes that represented their biggest pageant victories.

Sitting in the middle of the cheering section for Miss Kansas, surrounded by cardboard daisies on wooden sticks with Miss Kansas's face in the center and shouts of "You go girl!" I felt as if I were at a political convention or a religious revival. Also marooned in the Miss Kansas section, without any daisies, were a little girl, her mother (who had twice competed in the Miss Nevada state pageant), and her grandmother, who sat in front of me. The twelve-year-old watched the Pageant with wide eyes the whole night. She wore no crown or sash, but she looked smart in a black velvet dress.

After the talent segment, the girl turned to me and asked, "When I'm in the Miss America Pageant, I want to play the piano and the saxophone for my talent. I can switch back and forth. Do you think that would work?"

"Well, it would certainly be different," I replied.

"Good, then that would help me win."

"So, you really want to be Miss America someday?"

The girl nodded her head, her face solemn. Before replying, I paused. "Well, you can do that. But, you know, there are so many other things to do besides being a beauty queen."

The little girl did not hear me. She was rapturously watching as Miss Oklahoma was crowned Miss America 2006. All the other girls in the audience, those with crowns and those without, stood together, mouthing the words to the famous theme song as the new Miss America was serenaded by the voice of the great Pageant emcee, Bert Parks, who died in 1992: *"There she is, Miss America, there she is, your ideal. . . ."*

Miss America remains a part of our cultural landscape, both by clinging to tradition and by trying to take baby steps forward into the 21st century.

As I sat down in front of my television to watch the 2007 Pageant and the Pageant School special, I wondered what all those girls thought this year. Did they still aspire to be beauty queens, let alone Miss America? The previous month, December 2006, Miss USA Tara Conner rocked the pageant world with stories of alcohol and cocaine-influenced partying. The owner of the pageant, Donald Trump, made further headlines when he allowed Tara to keep her crown if she went into rehab—sparking a publicity-grabbing feud with Rosie O'Donnell.

Miss USA, part of the Miss Universe organization, is the sexier, and slightly tawdry, cousin to the Miss America Pageant. Miss Universe got its start in 1951, after Miss America Yolande Betbeze refused to be crowned in her swimsuit. Her decision led bathing suit company Catalina to pull its sponsorship and start its own pageant—today the Miss Universe system. This system does not include a talent component, and contestants are rewarded with mink coats and diamond jewelry instead of academic scholarships. The ratings for Miss USA/Universe are higher than for Miss America, not only because Trump's pageants have retained network affiliation, but also because they are clearly, and unapologetically, beauty pageants. Yet, Miss America remains a part of our cultural landscape, both by clinging to tradition and by trying to take baby steps forward into the 21st century.

The Miss USA scandals of 2006, including the dethroning of Miss Nevada due to racy photos on the Internet, highlighted the differences between Miss USA and Miss America. Miss USA might pose for the cover of *Playboy*, but Miss America makes pancakes as part of National Pancake Day. A Miss USA crown holds the promise of fame like that of Anna Nicole Smith, whereas the Miss America crown might help you become the wife of a Southern politician. Both push a certain type of femininity that still exists—though there are clear differences, as the women featured on CMT's Pageant School special can explain. Who knows, perhaps they might have a daughter in the Miss America pageant and a son in the Superbowl someday.

Beauty Pageants Thrive in Many Cultures Around the World

Rosie Goldsmith

Rosie Goldsmith is a journalist who reports regularly for the BBC, National Public Radio, Deutsche Welle, *and* Deutschland-funk *news organizations.*

Beauty pageants are a worldwide phenomenon with local character. In many parts of the world, the pageants are sustained by the money they make and the tourism they attract. The beauty industry is a big reason for the flourishing of beauty pageants. Women around the world compete in beauty pageants to get ahead in life and to show national pride. Feminist concerns about the exploitative nature of beauty pageants do not seem to be an issue for most participants.

"And you gotta recall, Miss Rosie," Jessica Tucker tells me in her *Ya-Ya Sisterhood* voice, "that this is a scholarship programme and we are all professional ladies." Tucker, Miss Watermelon, is competing in the Miss Louisiana beauty pageant for the fifth time, and "failure" is a dirty word. (They call it "failing forward".) Miss Louisiana is one of the US-wide preliminary state heats for the coveted Miss America, to be held in January 2006. For this one contest you may train for up to a year, up to 16 hours a day. Tucker is indeed a professional—a qualified electrical engineer. She is also an excellent pianist and has been able to get herself through college with her beauty pageant winnings. The pretty, athletic 22-year-old has been "pageanting" for several years. The reigning Miss Louisiana, I discover, started at 18 months old. "We prime the boys for soccer and baseball, and our daughters for pageants," her doting mum explains. "And here in the South, we *love* our pageants."

Beauty Pageants Around the World

In politically correct Britain, beauty contests are an apologetic, backstreet industry, but they still flourish elsewhere: my beauty odyssey for Radio 4 took me from Louisiana in the US to Sun City in South Africa and Hangzhou in China. All the competitions I saw were buoyed by eager corporate and community sponsors and undimmed by feminism, anti-racism and falling TV ratings. Beauty pageants are lucrative for the hotel and restaurant trades, as well as for the beauty and fashion industries. In China, the sole reason given for the enormous, extravagant Miss Tourism Queen International pageant was to promote tourism and "the beauty of China" in the city of Hangzhou, in east China's Zhejiang Province. It was the same story with Miss Louisiana and the Face of Africa in Sun City: beauty as a calling card for tourism. Beauty pageants mirror the state of a nation: its economy, its ambition, its self-image.

The modern beauty competition was born in the US. The world's market leader, the country holds in the region of 3,500 contests a year, from Miss Chicken Drumsticks to the spectacular, lavish, celebrity-driven circuses of Miss America and Miss USA (the latter is part-owned by Donald Trump). Miss America started off in Atlantic City in 1921 as a showcase for both beauty and tourism. The first contests were seedy affairs, but they were soon touched by Hollywood glamour and, during the Second World War, became patriotic, respectable and a particularly American form of upward mobility. (It wasn't until 1984, however, that the first black Miss America—Vanessa Williams—was crowned, after decades of protest.)

Beauty pageants mirror the state of a nation: its economy, its ambition, its self-image.

In China, pageants remain a novelty. After years of official disapproval—in the 1950s, Chairman Mao called them "bourgeois nonsense"—they only really took off in 2003, with the arrival of Miss World in its new home of uncritical capitalism. Today, pageants in China can't be big or brash enough. They are an integral part of the country's huge beauty industry, which is the fourth-largest growth area in China after cars, real estate and tourism. Paul French, a market analyst in Shanghai, observes: "Pageants are a sign that China has arrived on the world stage and can match the US."

In the new multiracial, inclusive South Africa, I was astonished to find there were no white finalists at all in the Face of Africa. The message these days is "black empowerment". The slick and splashy competition was a conscious display of black music, black fashion designers and black beauty—a backlash against the apartheid years, when even beauty contests were segregated.

The Reasons for Beauty Pageants

Beauty pageant finals tend to be vast, frenzied affairs. In nations without royalty, the winners can become queens, elevated and idealised far beyond their often humble beginnings. One Face of Africa hopeful had taken a four-hour bus ride from her village and stood for hours in the baking sun for the auditions.

But why do these women push themselves so hard? The answers were always the same: "To get a better life",

"To become a TV star/get a job in fashion", "To travel" and "I'm doing this for my country".

Each of the 30 Miss Louisiana finalists won cash towards college fees, while Miss America 2005, Deidre Downs, received $50,000. In China, the monetary prize is small, but you have the chance to travel and promote tourism. This year's Face of Africa winner, Kaone Kario, received a three-year modelling contract, clothes, free flights, make-up, a holiday, mobile phones: big prizes for any girl.

The girls were little more than pretty bridesmaids in a big national branding campaign.

So has feminism given up on the beauty contest? Wherever I raised the issue of exploitation, or pornography, or victimisation, people looked at me quizzically. Today's beauty queens were born long after the 1960s when feminists called for pageants to be banned.

"How can you be happy for your daughter to be lusted over in public?" I asked Byron, the Methodist minister father of Katherine Putnam, one of the Louisiana finalists, after watching her scissor-walk across stage in her revealing swimsuit. "That," Byron said, "is the problem for the observer, not for us. Beauty is not evil. Katherine eats well. She works out. She has a healthy body: those are good things to promote in our society. If she wins, she'd be a role model for others."

At the end of my odyssey I felt I'd been at a month-long wedding: uplifted but rather sick on the excess of glitter and gaiety. The girls were little more than pretty bridesmaids in a big national branding campaign. In South Africa, village girls plucked from obscurity have been launched on the international modelling stage, to become, as one judge told me, "our own African Kate Moss". In China, I found the 70 contestants in Miss Tourism Queen International desperate for the whole shambolic event to end. They'd been travelling through the country as "tourism ambassadors" for nearly a month. They'd lost weight, and their frocks and sashes were grubby. The contest organiser, however, was unsympathetic: "Being a beauty queen is a job and they have to treat it like training for the Olympics. With discipline."

3

Beauty Pageants Give Women of Many Cultures a Voice

Hammasa Kohistani

Hammasa Kohistani was the first Muslim to be crowned Miss England, in 2005. She represented England in the 2005 Miss World beauty pageant but failed to make the semifinal.

It seemed unlikely that a minority contestant in the English beauty pageant could win the title of Miss England, but that is what happened. The media portrayal of Muslims in Great Britain perpetuates many stereotypes, and this case was no different. However, pageants are one way for women of all kinds to have their voices heard and start to change inaccurate perceptions of minority groups, such as Muslims.

A year ago, I was just a student living in Norwood Green, an area in the west of London. My family is Muslim. Mum and Dad are from Afghanistan, but I was born in Uzbekistan. We lived in Kabul until I was five, and then in Russia and the Ukraine until I was nine, at which point we moved to England. I live in a brick house on a quiet street. Most of what I remember about my life is from London—I've always considered England my home.

One day, out of the blue, I received a letter saying I had to show up for rehearsals for the new Asian-themed Miss Maya pageant, held in West London. (When the British say "Asian," they mean Indians, Afghans, and Pakistanis.) My best friend,

Geeta, said, "Oh, it was me. I entered you in the contest as a surprise." Honestly, I thought it was all a joke. Although I've been modeling since I was fifteen, I never thought to enter any kind of contest. Pageants are a big deal among Asians, ever since Aishwarya Rai won Miss World, then became this huge Bollywood star. But I didn't even know minorities could enter English beauty contests!

Afghan women have been stereotyped and there's such controversy in the West over Islam—yet there I was, England's beauty queen.

There were lots of experienced pageant girls at Miss Maya who knew what to do and where to go. There were 27 contestants, selected from about 150 entries. For one section, I wore a sequined lilac-colored lengha, a sort of Indian skirt and .blouse with a scarf. I knew how to move in front of a camera from my modeling, and so I just went with that and won! I was automatically entered into the Miss England pageant, which was three months later. I took a few belly-dance lessons to prepare beforehand for my talent routine. There were 40 Miss England contestants—and a lot were really experienced. So I went in telling myself I'd just have fun. I didn't think I had any chance of winning. Asian parents tend to be a bit overprotective, but my mum and dad have always let me do as I wish, with the understanding that I must act responsibly and that I will go to university. (Education is a big deal in my family.) But Mum's also very stylish, and when I was entered into the Miss England pageant, she was so proud.

My memory of winning Miss England is a blur. After they announced that I won, Sarah Mendly, Miss Nottingham, hugged me and whispered, "It's you!" and pushed me toward the microphone. I told myself, Okay, I need to walk straight, smile at the camera, and not trip over my dress. Later, I thought, Wow, what have I achieved? Afghan women have been stereotyped and there's such controversy in the West over Islam—yet there I was, England's beauty queen.

But after I won Miss England, the press got my story all wrong. The interest in my religion was so extreme. In interviews it's always about me being Muslim. The *Times* in London reported that I've received death threats, which is not true! The press also reported that Muslim clerics were against me, which was blown out of proportion. I've tried to say in so many interviews, "Can you not write that because it's wrong?" But because it's already been published, they keep reprinting it.[1]

It seems the British press want to portray Muslims in a certain way, so they make it sound as if I'm from this awful, uneducated background—I'm not. My father has a degree in engineering. My mother has a master's in law, and used to be a lecturer at a university in Afghanistan. The BBC reported that my mother made the dress in which I won Miss England—suggesting that we're impoverished, which we aren't. I have also received criticism for not being "English" enough, meaning I don't have pale skin or blonde hair. But I consider myself British. I have almost no memories of Afghanistan. I can't really even remember much about living in Russia.

Pageants are not against feminism. They are stepping-stones for girls, a chance for us to have our voices heard.

Not many Asian models make it into the mainstream media in Britain. We tend to stick to Asian magazines. The biggest reason is cultural: Most of us feel better in clothes that don't show skin. In modeling, you sometimes must wear revealing clothing—and you won't get very far unless you're willing to do it. But because I'm Miss England, I'm now able to tell photographers if I'm not comfortable in an outfit, and they'll listen.

And one of the upsides of modern beauty pageants is that you decide what to wear. You don't have to parade around in a bikini if you don't want to. (I chose to wear a sarong over my swimsuit.) Pageants are not against feminism. They are stepping-stones for girls, a chance for us to have our voices heard. I feel like speaking out will allow me to make a difference, to be influential. And I want to make the most of this unique experience. —As told to Laurel Maury

Notes

1. The *Times* was unwilling to comment on their claim that Hammasa received death threats, citing editorial policy. The *Times* also quoted Akbar Ali, former chairman of the Islamic Society of Liverpool, as being against pageants. Ali, when reached, said that while beauty pageants are against Islamic ethos, he had never spoken against the current Miss England and was unaware that she is Muslim.

4

Beauty Pageants Show That Women Still Have Not Achieved Equality

Jill Filipovic

Jill Filipovic is a writer and lawyer based in New York City.

Beauty pageants like the Miss USA contest are a reflection of a culture in which women are not equal. In particular, women's bodies are not their own but are seen as objects of beauty for others. This perception of women's function and value in society is reflected in beauty pageants, but it did not arise from them. Beauty pageants will go away once the oppression of women and misogyny in larger society is eliminated.

In my least favorite line of an otherwise enjoyable movie, Dwayne in *Little Miss Sunshine* says, "You know what? F--- beauty contests. Life is one f---ing beauty contest after another. School, then college, then work. . . . F--- that."

The Miss USA pageant is airing tonight and I'm tempted to forgo thorough feminist analysis in favor of Dwayne's simple sentiment: F--- *that*. Because dated as it may be, the Miss USA pageant continues to serve as an indicator of just how far we haven't come.

Women and Beauty

The feminist arguments against beauty pageants are obvious, and have been around even before the famous 1968 demonstrations at the Miss America pageant in Atlantic City, which

Jill Filipovic, "Miss USA Pageant: How Far We Haven't Come," *Huffington Post*, March 23, 2007. Reproduced by permission.

spawned that impossible-to-kill myth of feminist bra-burning. But in 2007, when women are attending college and grad school in record numbers, when the first female Speaker of the House [U.S. representative Nancy Pelosi] is in power, and when women have unprecedented access to almost all professional fields, why are we still playing dress-up for money?

Despite achieving simple legal equality, women still lag behind when it comes to the higher-up positions in business, law, academia and politics. Our basic right to bodily autonomy is on the chopping block, as more anti-choice legislation and jurisprudence is introduced every year, sending the very strong message that our bodies are not just ours. Beauty is still one of the most valued characteristics a woman can have, and images of beautiful women bombard us every day. Is it any surprise that, in a culture which views women as objects to look at and vessels for reproduction, women will try to use the emphasis on their bodies to their own benefit?

The Miss USA pageant continues to serve as an indicator of just how far we haven't come.

Women are not stupid. We are rational actors who respond accordingly to our environments. From the time we're little girls, we're bombarded with images that reflect a very narrow standard of female beauty, and emphasize the idea that beauty (or at least the attempt to be beautiful) is a basic requirement of successful womanhood. If you happen to be blessed with the features that are culturally idealized (whiteness and thinness, among others), why not use it and make some money off of what so many other women do for free, and to feel good about yourself to boot?

Certainly plenty of women like dressing up, and like the ritual of putting on make-up and doing their hair and feeling pretty. Wanting to be perceived as attractive is no great sin, and isn't strictly a woman's concern. The difference, though, is that being attractive is considered much more important for women than it is for men, and women are required to spend much more time, effort and money on their physical appearance. While marketers are no doubt trying to breed male insecurity in order to push more product, women still dominate when it comes to the purchase of beauty-related goods. Women still spend millions on make-up, hair care, and lotions and potions claiming to do everything from eliminate wrinkles to get rid of cellulite to plump up breasts and lips. Women still make up most of the plastic surgeries performed each year. Women still account for the vast majority of people with eating disorders. Woman are still the primary funders of the diet industry.

The Miss USA pageant is not, by any stretch, good for feminism or good for women as a class.

Beauty Pageants Reflect Contemporary Culture

There is no shame in being one of the millions of American women who live in this culture and who structure their lives accordingly. I'm one of them. So are the women in the Miss USA pageant. Feminists have been leveling thorough and valid criticisms at beauty contests and consumer beauty culture for more than 40 years, and yet the contests persist. Women continue to participate in them, and we continue to watch them on TV. It's no big mystery as to why: Beauty contest participants reap great financial benefits when they win, and American viewers are fully accustomed to evaluating and watching women for pleasure.

Ideally, beauty contests will eventually go the way of the dodo. The Miss USA pageant is not, by any stretch, good for feminism or good for women as a class. But it's not happening in a vacuum. For 40 years, feminists have been arguing that pageants are a small part of a larger-scale system of oppression which positions women's bodies as objects to serve others—to give them pleasure, to make them money, to sell their product, to birth their baby. While many Americans have duly noted beauty pageants to be silly and outdated, we often fail to recognize how they operate within a greater context of generalized and widely accepted misogyny.

The norms that these contests promote are unfortunately not nearly as obsolete as many of us would like to believe, and pageants continue to serve as a reflection of contemporary culture—one in which we pay lip service to women's rights, but focus more on how good women look in a bathing suit. If we actually want to move on from beauty contests, we need to tackle the broader problems of positioning women as consumable products, state attempts at controlling female sexuality, and the continued marginalization of women in the workplace. We need to drop the obsession with women's bodies and with what women do with their reproductive organs. In a nutshell, we need to recognize that women are human beings worthy of full human rights, and that we are not decorations or vessels or servants.

We're on the path to equality, but there's still a long road ahead. And since I'm pretty sure we aren't going to get there by tonight, I'll be spending this evening reading a book.

5

There's Nothing Wrong with Beauty Pageants

Wendy McElroy

Wendy McElroy is a writer who considers herself an individualist feminist and individualist anarchist. She is the editor of the book Liberty for Women: Freedom and Feminism in the Twenty-first Century.

Most feminists are upset by the presence of beauty pageants. Their claim that the contests objectify women and cause violence is flawed. Additionally, their concern about oppressive beauty standards is misguided—many kinds of beauty are valued in society and women who compete in particular beauty pageants do so freely. Beauty contests are harmless contests that applaud beauty in much the same way that college exams applaud intelligence. Feminists should not be concerned about beauty pageants.

A beauty contest at Lakehead University [in Ontario, Canada] aroused sharp protest from campus feminists.

Feminist Anger About Beauty Contests

The flap came on the heels of a similar contest at which I applauded from the audience. The contrast made me wonder: "Why are politically correct feminists so upset by beauty pageants?"

"Upset" may be too tame a word. Rage against beauty contests lies at the very roots of PC [politically correct] feminism.

Wendy McElroy, "In Defense of Beauty Pageants," *ifeminists.com*, November 17, 2004. Reproduced by permission.

Indeed, a high-profile protest at the 1968 Miss America beauty contest is often credited with bringing the feminist movement into public awareness.

It was a defining moment, with feminist protesters setting off stink bombs and singing, "Ain't she sweet; making profits off her meat."

Beauty contests have evolved since 1968. For example, the majority of judges at the Lakehead pageant were female; there was a female "co-host"; 40 percent of the tickets went to women. But PC attacks have not substantially altered.

Some of the Lakehead debate revolved around the appropriateness of holding a beauty contest at the on-campus pub; that's a valid debate. But mere inappropriateness doesn't explain why feminists campaigned so vigorously to cancel the event despite the fact that the breach of contract would have resulted in a fine of $50,000 to $155,000 to be paid by the university.

It is not clear why a celebration of female physical beauty is sexist ... especially when all the women involved are eager to participate.

The Objectification Argument

The rhetoric surrounding their campaign offers a stereotypical example of feminism's stock-in-trade arguments against beauty contests, on-campus or off.

In the Lakehead student newspaper, Angie Gollat of the on-campus Gender Issues Centre (GIC) lambastes the event as "sexist" and "heterosexist." It is difficult to imagine campus feminists objecting to lesbian events because they are "homosexist." But hypocrisy aside, it is not clear why a celebration of female physical beauty is sexist—that is, anti-woman—especially when all the women involved are eager to participate.

In the same newspaper, unidentified students state their concerns that "the objectification of women [that is, the contest] leads to violence against women."

There are two problems with that argument. Being judged on the basis of your beauty is no more "objectification" than taking a college exam and being judged on your intellect; yet, as far as I know, every student will take exams. Moreover, absolutely no data supports a connection between beauty pageants and violence against women.

Indymedia carried the GIC's call for a protest, which read, "Concerned citezens [sic] are staging an anti-corporate demonstration," to show "that discriminatory events are not welcome on campus."

The anti-corporate remark refers to the pageant's sponsor and merely reflects left-wing bias. (Tax-funded feminists are notoriously contemptuous of the free market.) And, unless a particular race or religion was barred from entry, the charge of discrimination doesn't make sense. The contest was "women only," but so are women's sports and many feminist events.

Concerns About Beauty Standards

Two more substantial arguments underlie the demonization of beauty contests. One was presented in a 1991 book that caused a phenomenon upon publication: *The Beauty Myth: How Images of Beauty Are Used Against Women* by Naomi Wolf.

Wolf hypothesizes a cause-and-effect relationship between women's liberation and society's ideal of beauty. Although women have advanced, Wolf contends that, "in terms of how we feel about ourselves physically, we may actually be worse off than our unliberated grandmothers."

Why? Because of how "cruelly images of female beauty have come to weigh upon us."

In short, the ideal of female beauty oppresses modern women in a manner presumably not experienced by earlier generations. Thus, feminist Jo Freeman writes of the 1968 protest, "All women were made to believe they were inferior because they couldn't measure up to Miss America beauty standards."

By this analysis, beauty contestants become symbols and tools of oppression.

The analysis is deeply flawed. For one thing, society has no one standard of beauty. A cursory scan of today's "beautiful people" reveals women of all ages and ethnic groups, with no one body type or style of dress.

Moreover, the beauty of one woman doesn't force another to conform. My favorite makeup is a scrubbed face and I wear no-brand blue jeans. All the women I know are intelligent enough to make such decisions for themselves.

Envy Veiled as Unfairness

Yet the argument that beauty contests are unfair to the average woman is common. An influential book by the philosopher John Rawls became popular in left-wing circles and lends the argument support. Rawls' book, "A Theory of Justice," contends, "no one deserves his place in the distribution of natural endowments, any more than one deserves one's initial starting place in society."

It is time to lighten up and applaud beauty, not pathologize it.

To Rawls, naturally beautiful people are akin to those born rich or with perfect health; they have won "the social lottery." That is, they've benefited from random luck, which they did not earn or deserve. His theory has been used to justify the redistribution of wealth and power in society.

And one way to "redistribute" natural beauty is to pathologize its display.

The feminist contention that beauty contests are unfair to the average woman has a Rawlsian ring. It also sounds like envy.

Even after the Lakehead beauty contest had passed, the GIC made a declaration of war, "This is a wake up call to all you dormant egalitarians. It's time to mobilize."

Actually it is time to lighten up and applaud beauty, not pathologize it.

6

Beauty Pageants Perpetuate Myths About Female Beauty

Beth Dalbey

Beth Dalbey, a former reporter for Iowa newspaper, is currently communications editor for the Great Ape Trust.

Although beauty pageants have changed since the first demonstrations against them in the 1960s—placing more emphasis on scholarships—they are still symbols of the exploitation of women. Beauty pageants are becoming less popular but not, unfortunately, because women have no need to rely on their looks to get ahead; rather, the waning interest appears to be because the pageants are not sexy enough. Beauty pageants perpetuate many of the unrealistic beauty standards that make women insecure, causing them to seek out expensive beauty treatments and surgeries.

The irony was so delicious I almost poked my own eye out in a hilarious fit of laughter the other morning while getting ready for work. The television was on in the living room and the newscaster had just passed along the dreadful news that that Zuleyka Rivera Mendoza, Miss Puerto Rico, had collapsed under the weight of her all-metal chain-link dress shortly after she was crowned Miss Universe on July 23 [2006].

Women in Chains

In that one defining moment, she emerged as a perfect metaphor for a tradition that shackles women. Sadly, though, it's a better bet that she chose a chain-link dress because she's a

Beth Dalbey, "Women in Chains," *Business Record*, vol. 24, no. 31, July 31, 2006, p. 17. Reproduced by permission.

fashionista, not because she wanted to make a political statement about how pageants exploit women and reduce them to a set of measurements and an all-American-girl answer to a silly question. After all, who doesn't want world peace?

(And, though it's not nice to say, the fact that fashion trumped common sense shows that pageants are more about beauty than brains. With white-hot stage lights heating up her skin-tight metal dress, it should hardly have been surprising that she fainted.)

Beauty pageants have changed a lot since 1968, when demonstrators protested the Miss America beauty pageant in Atlantic City for parading women like cattle at a state fair to show off their physical attributes. The idea that pageants don't objectify women is still a tough sell, but at least more emphasis has been placed on scholarships—that is, until last year when ABC dropped the Miss America pageant due to sagging ratings and it was relegated to a minor cable channel, Country Music Television.

The idea that pageants don't objectify women is still a tough sell.

Don't get too excited. The bad news in what appeared to be good news is truly grim. Lisa Ades, who directed the Public Broadcasting Service documentary "Miss America," said in an interview last year with the *Washington Post* that though the Miss America pageant may have run its course, its audience may have waned more because "it's simply not sexy enough" than because a beauty pageant is no longer necessary to help women get ahead.

The Beauty in Beauty Pageants

Beauty and feminism are not mutually exclusive. Women don't have to wear beefy shoes and loose-fitting jumpers to be considered feminists, and The Feminist Majority isn't a group of unattractive women who can't get dates. Beauty pageants, even as they focus more on social issues than ever before, keep those myths alive, however. That takes some of the curiosity out of studies that show American women are less confident about their body images today than at any other time in history.

The subjects chosen by Italian artist Giorgione, whose portraits of voluptuous, curvy women in the 1500s helped define the standard for nudes, resemble today's average-sized woman, yet many of us are anorexic-thin (happily, I am not in this group). Advertising campaigns by companies such as Dove featuring "real women" are attempting to change this, but are receiving mixed reviews from those who want women in the underwear to be model-thin. It's a national obsession. Cosmetic surgery in this country is a $9.4 billion annual industry, and if a surgeon can't fix it, it can be smoothed out with a Botox injection or sucked out surgically. We wax our legs, pluck our eyebrows, get our tummies tucked and spend about $30 billion annually on diet schemes.

American women are less confident about their body images today than at any other time in history.

This is liberation?

Don't get me wrong. I'd sooner give up my subscription to *Ms.* magazine than a provocative pair of shoes, even when the V-shaped toe box squeezes my toes to numbness and the stiletto heels bring on leg cramps. I don't mean to preach. After all, when I almost poked out my own eye, it was a mascara wand I was wielding.

7

Beauty Pageants Are Full of Scandals

Mark Schwed

Mark Schwed is a staff writer for Palm Beach Post.

Once a major event, the Miss America pageant has become just another reality show. The Miss America pageant claims that the beauty queens in the pageant are to be emulated, but a long history of scandals challenges that claim. From scandals within the pageant, including acts of sabotage between contestants, to scandals outside, including posing nude for magazines, beauty pageants have always had a scandalous dark side.

Miss America represents the highest ideals. She is a real combination of beauty, grace, and intelligence, artistic and refined. She is a type which the American Girl might well emulate.

If that mission statement from Miss America's Web site is true, God help us.

The beauty pageant industry is reeling from a slew of scandals that involve drugs, drunks, topless romps, blackmailers and saboteurs.

How appropriate, then, that the most prestigious and squeaky-clean pageant of them all—Miss America—will crown its new queen on Saturday in a city that boasts of its sinful pleasures: Las Vegas. At a casino, no less. . . .

Mark Schwed, "The Ugly Side of Beauty Pageants," *Palm Beach Post*, January 25, 2008, p. 1E. Reproduced by permission.

Is it any wonder that Americans have soured on the whole beauty queen deal? With ratings nose-diving year after year, what once was a major television event has now become a cheesy reality show.

The beauty pageant industry is reeling from a slew of scandals that involve drugs, drunks, topless romps, black-mailers and saboteurs.

The big broadcast networks have abandoned the Miss America pageant due to lack of interest. Instead, the pageant will air live on a cable network that used to be known as The Learning Channel, but now goes by TLC—"the only television network dedicated to lifelong learning for viewers who want to grow up, not old."

To pump up interest, TLC had to do something. So it forced the 52 contestants to live together under one roof for a month before the competition. With elements of *America's Next Top Model*, *Project Runway*, *How Do I Look?*, *Big Brother* and *Survivor*, the competitors from each state are harangued about their hair, their clothes, and their talents in *Miss America Reality Check*.

"Bye bye hair spray and caked-on makeup," is the story line for one episode, where the women are put through an "it girl" boot camp to rid them of their old-fashioned ways and looks. In another bit, each contestant must carry a martini glass filled with liquid over a seesaw—practice for that future DUI stop?

There is one more change. For the first time, viewers of *Miss America Reality Check* will get a chance to vote for their favorite, with the winner getting a guaranteed spot in the final 10 for Saturday's finale, which airs at 8 p.m. on TLC.

But the ugly side of beauty pageants will be fresh in viewers minds.

Last week, at the Miss South Florida Fair pageant in suburban West Palm Beach, someone used deep red metallic lipstick to smear four stripes, 3 to 4 feet long, on the backside of Jessica Wittenbrink's $3,400 Sherri Hill rhinestone and silk taffeta gown.

"Whoever did it ground it into the fabric, like they were angry," says Robin Fleming of Wellington, who sold the dress to Wittenbrink and then worked frantically backstage to clean up the mess.

Tears welled up in Wittenbrink's eyes, but she soldiered on and won the title. Within 48 hours, she was telling her tale on NBC's *Today*. Tragedy makes good TV.

Twenty-five years ago, Fleming was a beauty queen.

"I competed with Halle Berry when she won Miss Ohio USA. I was one of the finalists—Miss Dayton, Ohio," she says. "I have never seen something like this. You hear things. You hear about people being bitter after a pageant. Or complaining about how things are run. There are always urban legends about girls who would take scissors to a gown. But that's what they are—urban legends. I have never seen a deliberate act of sabotage."

Never say never.

Scandal at beauty pageants is nothing new.

Scandals Are Nothing New

Just a few months ago, Ingrid Marie Rivera claimed someone put pepper spray on her gown, causing her to swell up and break out in hives during the Miss Puerto Rico contest. She still won and will compete in the Miss Universe pageant this year.

No word on whether pageant organizers will erect metal detectors at the dressing room door to keep out the fashion saboteurs.

Of course, scandal at beauty pageants is nothing new.

The first big fall from grace occurred in 1973 when Miss World, Marjorie Wallace, had to turn in her crown after just four months for dating swivel-hipped singer Tom Jones and other well-known people. Her punishment? She went on to have a nice career in television, including a stint on *Entertainment Tonight*.

In 1984, it was Vanessa Williams who had to give up her Miss America crown after nude pictures of her were published in *Penthouse*. Her tears were replaced by joy as she launched a successful singing and acting career. She can be seen today playing a fashion diva on the hit ABC show *Ugly Betty*.

Apparently, it's good to be bad. But it's also bad to be good.

In the most absurd scandal of all, in 2002, Miss Universe, Oxana Fedorova of Russia, was fired for missing too many events. Her excuse: She didn't want to interrupt her law school education to shill for the pageant. So much for brains over beauty.

Apparently, it's good to be bad.

But in the last two years, beauty pageant meltdowns have exploded in the news.

In 2006, Miss USA Tara Conner, a sweet girl from Kentucky, moved into New York City's Trump Place apartments and immediately became a girl gone wild. There were allegations of drinking, cocaine use and sexual escapades. Donald Trump, who owns the Miss USA brand, gave her a reprieve, as long as she went to rehab and accepted drug testing.

Triumphant Return

She emerged from her stint in rehab, professing to be clean and sober, a better person for having gone through it all. Her tearful return to the pageant was a triumphant affair.

New Jersey has its share of problem girls.

Ashley Harder, Miss New Jersey USA, bowed out of the Miss USA pageant after she became pregnant. There was the case of Amy Polumbo, Miss New Jersey, who claimed someone was trying to blackmail her by threatening to release her racy photos. To head them off at the pass, she went public and revealed the photos—on the *Today* show.

And finally, there was Katie Rees, Miss Nevada USA, who was stripped of her tiara by Trump after a series of raunchy photos surfaced on the Internet.

The lucrative offers came rolling in. The aspiring actress turned down nude romps in *Girls Gone Wild* and *Playboy*. Finally, she got her dream job.

She just inked a $2 million deal to work—where else—at a Vegas casino.

8

Beauty Pageants in Prison Can Have Positive Effects

Jean Trounstine

Jean Trounstine is professor of humanities at Middlesex Community College in Massachusetts. She taught literature, writing, and drama at Framingham Women's Prison for ten years.

Beauty pageants for prisoners are developing all over the world, from Russia to Kenya to Columbia. Despite legitimate feminist concerns about beauty pageants in the United States since the 1960s, beauty pageants in prison do not necessarily present the same problems for women as pageants outside of prison, and can actually offer many benefits to female inmates. Beauty contests in prison can provide educational opportunities, boost self-confidence, and offer a break from the challenge of prison life.

Picture this: a prison camp in Siberia with 2,000 inmates, twenty miles outside of Novosibirsk, the third largest city in Russia. The women wake at 5:45 for eight hours of sewing police uniforms in the textile factory. They walk across the yard, wrapped for the cold in wool as drab and gray as the sky. There's no hot water. They subsist on a diet of mashed peas and bread.

The Prison Beauty Pageant

Now jump to this: an auditorium filled with two hundred people. Balloons decorate the stage. The steps to the podium are newly carpeted. It's the same camp, but during the annual

Jean Trounstine, "Ms. Captivity," *The Women's Review of Books*, vol. 25, no. 2, March–April 2008, pp. 18–19. Reproduced by permission.

Miss Spring contest. Behind the scenes, nine women, one selected by each cell block, anxiously prepare. For round one, the Greek Goddess, the camp's expert seamstresses turn their candidate into Mata Hari. Her bare skin shows above her low slung gold skirt; her breasts are barely covered with red and pink; her arms are wrapped in golden straps. In the Flower Round, another contestant wears a gown, again fashioned by her whole block, made of hundreds of white cloth flowers, each with a delicate yellow-and-green center. Her glittery makeup, pearls, and white shoes evoke Miss America, but her train speaks of weddings, New Year's floats, Cirque de Soleil.

Should feminists around the world shake in their boots?

Almost any activity, when you take it behind bars, acquires a new significance.

After all, in 1968, in one of the first actions of US feminism's second wave, protesters gathered in Atlantic City to picket the Miss America pageant and the false icons of beauty it presented. As some unfurled banners reading "Women's Liberation" inside the hall, others created street theatre outside, crowning a sheep and calling for the end to the oppression of women that the pageant made manifest. Carol Hanisch, who coined the phrase, "the personal is political," led the demonstrators in tossing what she called "instruments of female torture"—high heels, nylons, girdles, corsets, hair curlers, and false eyelashes—into a Freedom Trash Can. In a 2003 radio interview, Hanish credited fellow demonstrator Roz Baxandall with coming up with the action's best slogan: "Every day in a woman's life is a walking Miss America contest."

However, in Siberian Camp UF-91/9, a woman's day is anything but a beauty contest. There, dressing up and entering the world of the imagination can be treasured opportunities, respites from the rules and scarcity that usually dominate her life. Although the clichéd titles and the concepts of women the pageants promote may seem bizarre to those of us on the outside, almost any activity, when you take it behind bars, acquires a new significance.

The first prison beauty pageant in Siberia took place in 2000, the brainchild of an inmate. It began simply, with costumes created from everyday objects such as plastic bags and fake flowers. These days, the women work together for months before the pageant, which is hardly the competitive, individualistic event implied by the word "contest." Their interpretations of the themes assigned by the prison administration, such as Miss Spring, Miss Charm, and Miss Grace, are liberating and even, in some cases, downright subversive. Consider the irony of portraying an inmate as a pure lily with giant white calla spathes around her head, her slicked-back hair highlighting the flower's center, her trim body undulating sensually to form the stem.

Prisoner Participation

As a woman who grew up in the sixties, I used to consider endorsing any sort of beauty contest inconceivable—but that was before I saw two short documentaries about the pageants at Camp UF-91/9, *The Contest*, produced by the Polish journalist Zygmunt Dzieciolowski, and *Miss Gulag*, produced by Neihausen-Yatskova and Vodar Films. They show the contenders taking the runway by storm, cheered on by their peers, in a parody of the stale rigidity and lack of sexuality of traditional pageants. "You can be free anywhere, even in a dark cell," says one contestant, referring to her pageant experience. In *The Contest*, one woman adds a musical number to the Pageant's dress-up proceedings, packaging herself as a cabaret singer à la Sally Bowles. Commenting on her performance, Dzieciolowski says, "The brilliance in the women's handiwork is the opposite of the mass production of the factory."

Beauty pageants are now widespread in Russian prisons. Make up, gifts for the unit, and credits toward early release are the prizes. In Kyrgyzstan, the first contest behind bars in 2005 was juried by a group led by Tursunbai Bakir-uulu, the Kyrgyz human rights ombudsperson. He brought the competitors soap, detergents, booklets on legal issues, and stationary, and the winner received a television set, presumably to watch when she got out.

Yet, even though women themselves originated the pageants, it's fair to wonder whether the wardens are promoting them for public relations purposes, to boost the idea of a new Russia, devoid of unbearable gulags. At the screening of *Miss Gulag* I attended this summer in Baltimore, the Russian-American director Irina Yatskova said that in her experience, the prison was still excruciatingly bleak. Although she was allowed to film it, her crew had to sign forms saying they would stick within physical boundaries determined by the camp: no filming anywhere but in approved areas. If they strayed, they'd find themselves UF-91/9 prisoners instead of observers.

Administrators who endorse the contests claim that they "increase self-esteem."

Changing Prisoners' Lives

Beauty pageants are proliferating behind bars. They've been held all over the world: in Mexico, Brazil, Columbia, Peru, Venezuela, Uganda, Kenya, South Africa, Lithuania, and the US. Prison blogger Yraida, whose posted address in 2005 was a Florida federal prison camp, wrote that during the camp's Hispanic Heritage celebrations in September and October, 21 female prisoners, one to represent each Latin country, were selected to compete for the title of Miss Hispanic. Yraida posted a picture showing the costumes, "dresses designed and made by other prisoners . . . just gorgeous, long gowns with shoulderless backs . . . open midsection dresses with prison-made earrings and tiaras." Like her Russian counterparts, she feels that the pageant offers inmates some measure of freedom.

Although when I contacted the Florida federal prison camp, administrators denied that beauty contests ever take place inside, Yraida described how, in her federal prison experience, Black History Month and the Fourth of July were also celebrated with glorious pageants.

Administrators who endorse the contests claim that they "increase self-esteem." I have always winced at that term, perhaps because it seems too simplistic, a catchall. According to the BBC News, warden Wanini Kireri of Lang'ata, the largest women's prison in Kenya, organized a pageant for exactly that reason: to boost her charges' self-confidence. She had read an article about a pageant behind bars, and sought help from a local beauty college to dress the women in African designs and make them up for the contest. She said, "When I came to Lang'ata, I wanted to make a change. I did not want to get into the usual routine." The 26-year-old who became Miss Lang'ata exclaimed, "I feel good. I feel excited. Winning the pageant will change my life." After serving her sentence, she planned to take a hairdressing, modeling, and beauty course offered by the school that helped with the pageant. After that, she said, she might attend college.

Critics might justifiably wonder if hairdressing and modeling courses can really change a prisoner's life. But research shows that there is more at stake than beauty worship. Some pageants aim to train women so they get jobs upon release. The unemployment rate of women in Russia is seventy percent. According to Human Rights Watch, in Kenya women make up eighty percent of the agricultural labor force and provide sixty percent of farm income, yet they own only five percent of the land. For a Kenyan prisoner, a beauty school education may mean survival. Those who receive such opportunities may feel more confident in their abilities to achieve in other arenas, thus Miss Lang'ata's intention to "go to univer-

49

sity"—not insignificant, since female enrollment in universities is only thirty percent, according to Akili Dada, a nonprofit organization that supports Kenyan girls and women. In addition, it is well known that the more education a prisoner has, the less likely she is to return to crime.

In Latin America, reporters have said that beauty is a "national obsession." According to *USA Today* writer Toby Muse, in Colombia, "[a]nnual telecasts of the Miss World and Miss Universe competitions draw ratings on par with World Cup soccer matches." Women prisoners in Brazil and Colombia, like those in Kenya, participate in pageants to get time off their sentences, cash awards, or in some cases the chance to go to modeling school.

Some pageants aim to train women so they get jobs upon release.

Some Bad Apples

Rebecca Roth is a US citizen who has been incarcerated since February 2006 in the Puente Grande women's penitentiary in Mexico, where those arrested but not convicted can be held for years. She lives in the same cell with sentenced women. Cockroaches are not uncommon. Almost fifty, Roth came of age when questions about women's roles were freely in the air. She confirms the observation of Susan Dworkin, the author of *Miss America, 1945: Bess Myerson and the Year That Changed Our Lives*, that any beauty pageant has a "dark underbelly." Roth writes in an e-mail, "Even in the slammer women flirt with the male judges in order to gain favor." Contestants, many of whom are over fifty, some of whom cannot read or write and can barely sign their names, "practiced and practiced," says Roth, going over "their promenades, dance routines, and beauty pageant smiles." The women rehearsed musical numbers to "New York, New York," complete with "styrofoam top hats that we painted black with white bands," and to "Brazil." "The 'Brazil' girls were given multicolor tulle carioca skirts that tied on with colored bias tape and felt eye masks that they were told to decorate with sequins," says Roth. (Note that the prisoners were "told" to decorate.) "My moment of truth came where I realized the people in front of me were going to decide if I was queen material based on a dance routine and a walk in my tight blue dress," she says.

Still, she feels it was "absolutely worth it" to take part in Queen of the Prison, a contest held yearly for prisoners over age 36, because of "the additional liberty from the overcrowded cellblock after 6:00 PM curfew." For their efforts, participants were allowed to stay outside, sometimes until 8:00 or 9:00 pm. To gain any kind of liberty is precious when a life behind bars is defined, as Jean Harris says of her experience in New York's Bedford Hills, as having doors opened for you "ninety times a day." Roth's sister, who has moved to be near her in Mexico, writes that this year, Rebecca found some freedom in sewing and designing costumes for the pageant.

During the contests, prisoners grab a momentary respite from conditions that range from the austere to the intolerable.

Certainly some pageants exploit far more than they support. Questionable ones include a "voluntary" singing competition in Maricopa County, Arizona. The prison-based *American Idol*-like contest is run by the controversial sheriff Joe Arpaio, also known for forcing male prisoners to wear pink underwear, housing prisoners in tents in the desert, and bringing back chain gangs. A sleezy website called "Iowahawk" posts mug shots of women behind bars and, in a nearly pornographic announcement, encourages readers to vote for their favorite "Hoosegow Honey 2007." These are the kinds of exploitative pageants that led Carol Hanisch and other women's liberationists of the sixties to picket Miss America.

Nevertheless, prison beauty pageants also demonstrate the immense resourcefulness of women who are locked-up, who live day-in and day-out in cramped spaces, far from their children and other loved ones, without much to cheer about in their lives. During the contests, prisoners grab a momentary respite from conditions that range from the austere to the intolerable; they use their creativity and even gain a leg-up upon release. The women, even if not the pageants, broadcast loudly, with style and pizzazz, that beauty does not have to die in prison.

9

Beauty Pageant Winners Are Not Good Role Models

Kim Lunman

Kim Lunman is a writer and a reporter for Sun Media, Canada's largest newspaper publisher.

The scandals in 2006 involving Miss USA and Miss Teen USA are not isolated events for beauty queens. Although beauty pageant winners are often deemed to be good role models for young girls, they rarely live up to the myth. In reality, there is a long history of beauty queens who got in trouble for bad behavior as varied as posing nude, public drunkenness, and fighting. Beauty pageants are outdated and serve no positive social role; it is time that they come to an end.

Miss USA may be one of the few people Donald Trump hasn't fired. The reigning prince of publicity let the fallen beauty queen go to rehab with her tiara because he said he believes in second chances.

Beauty Pageant Hypocrisy

The Donald is wrong. There should be no second chances for Miss USA, period. And Tara Conner's party-girl antics are yet another reason why the outdated beauty pageant should be cancelled. Besides being shallow and sexist, it's a sham to prop up the image of the beauty queen as the most wholesome female role model in America. Why not just cancel and reintro-

Kim Lunman, "When Beauty Queens Go Bad," *National Post*, December 23, 2006, p. A22. Reproduced by permission.

duce the pageant as yet another reality television program, and call it Miss Behaving or Miss Demeanour, if things really get out of hand? Heck, liven up the talent portion of the competition with beer chugging and table dancing.

But Trump, owner of the Miss Universe Organization, which includes Miss USA and Miss Teen USA, would have us all believe this is a fairy tale about a princess named Miss Understood. He announced earlier this week that he would give Miss USA, a just turned 21-year-old blonde from Kentucky, another chance if she went to rehab following reports of drug abuse and drinking in New York during her reign. Conner bravely put on her sash at the same news conference and tearfully announced she still wants to be, like, the best Miss USA ever.

What a sob story. There's something incredibly hypocritical about a beauty pageant insisting it exists to provide role models for young girls when its queen is acting more like Britney Spears than royalty. Besides, what is the job anyway? Cutting a few ribbons, smiling and waving on parade floats, and being photographed with celebrities like Barbara Walters at black-tie galas. She wasn't much of a role model to Miss Teen USA, Katie Blair, who is also in trouble this week [December 17–23, 2006] for underage drinking and carousing with Miss USA in New York nightclubs. (Mothers Against Drunk Driving announced it is severing ties with 18-year-old Blair, a former spokesperson for the organization.)

It's a sham to prop up the image of the beauty queen as the most wholesome female role model in America.

Miss Canada was axed for being outdated in 1992 and maybe it's time Miss USA should take a cue from her northern neighbour and take off her sash for good.

All About Appearances

Conner isn't the first beauty queen to make headlines for bad behaviour—but at least she got to keep her tiara. Danielle House, a former Miss Newfoundland, lost her Miss Canada International title when she was convicted of assaulting her ex-boyfriend's girlfriend in a barroom catfight. Her notoriety led to a nude spread in Playboy magazine in 1997 with her posing in a pair of boxing gloves.

Miss USA 1983, Vanessa Williams, was dethroned when nude photographs of her surfaced. The controversy launched her career as a singer and actress.

The Miss USA pageant is a modern-day mirage machine.

It's not women parading on a stage in swimsuits that is offensive about Miss USA so much as organizers insisting contestants have excellent personalities and would actually be curing cancer if they weren't so busy twirling batons. Officials downplay the importance of appearance on the Miss USA Web site even though all the contestants look as though they just stepped off the assembly line at Mattel. Of course, looks matter. It's called a beauty pageant, not an ugly pageant, for a reason.

Trying to convince people that Miss USA is a role model for morality is like trying to argue domestic diva and convicted felon Martha Stewart represents minivan-driving homemakers in Wisconsin. Does anyone really believe the billionaire businesswoman cleans her own house? No. But that doesn't mean she isn't hawking her new Homekeeping Handbook in time for the holidays with helpful hints like how to glue broken plates back together and get red wine stains out of napkins.

Like the much-marketed image of Stewart as Queen Homekeeper, the Miss USA pageant is a modern-day mirage machine. Trump is no doubt counting on negative publicity to attract more viewers for the 2007 pageant to watch Conner pass on her tarnished tiara. Last year's pageant attracted the second-lowest viewership in the event's history.

Ironically, The Donald didn't give any second chances to Stewart when he fired her after one season of her own series of *The Apprentice*. But then she committed the ultimate sin: Lousy ratings. And that's a bad thing—even for Miss USA.

10

African Pageant Winners Can Enhance Their Nation's Image

Clayton Goodwin

Clayton Goodwin is a journalist who writes for a variety of publications worldwide, including the New African, *Great Britain's* The Guardian, *and Caribbean newspaper* Barbados Advocate.

African women involved in media offer a necessary perspective on world affairs, and African beauty pageant winners are in a similar position to provide a unique voice from a highly visible platform. The woman who represented Zambia in the Miss World pageant is an example of someone who has used her title in an exemplary way, encouraging others to follow in her footsteps. Beauty pageants around the world provide an opportunity for countries, through the female titleholders, to improve their profile worldwide by drawing attention to important national issues and promoting tourism.

For several years, a Zambian lady, Rosemary Chileshe, has been Britain's leading African beauty contestant and model, and her compatriots are succeeding now in all aspects of the industry—from promotion to participation.

African Women in Media

Yet beauty is not restricted to pageantry. Lukwesa Burak, a beauty in her own right, whom I had the pleasure of meeting at a reception for UK Zambians at the High Commission in

Clayton Goodwin, "Zambian Beauties Lead the Way," *New African*, vol. 467, November 2007, pp. 83–84. Reproduced by permission.

London, can be described in the nicest possible way as being a "lady of the night". She presents *Sky Late News* from midnight to 4 a.m. and then fronts *Sky World News*, which caters [to] audiences in Africa, Asia and Europe, until 6 a.m.

Lukwesa, whose working "day" starts when she leaves her home in Leicestershire for London at 7 p.m., has an affinity with the hours of darkness.

"I've always worked the early shift," she says. "At Nottingham (earlier in her career as a 'weather girl'), it was non-stop: we had 21 radio broadcasts in the morning. I had to be up at 4.30 a.m. to start at 6 a.m. First I had to ring the Weather Centre, where the forecasters would give you the science and you had to work out the best way to put the story across to the public."

Lukwesa can still remember being "a little girl, freshly bathed, pony-tailed, and in her new dress sitting in a puddle making mud cakes" back in Zambia, where she was born and which she left aged eight years when her mother remarried.

Rosemary Chileshe's career has provided a blueprint for what a beauty title and its holder should be.

She arrived in Britain during one of the worst winters on record. She graduated from Sussex University with a degree in Geography and European Studies, and was awarded a European Union Scholarship to complete a Master of Science degree at Leicester University. Her studies included a year at Neuchatel in Switzerland through which she became fluent in French.

She joined *Sky News* last year from being a news anchor for *BBC East Midlands Today* after working on various local radio stations. Her broadcasting career started at the *BBC* Weather Centre before moving into news presentation. She has been able to "break the news" on several leading international stories, including the execution of Saddam Hussein,

Israel's invasion of Lebanon and the Gaza Strip, North Korea's first nuclear test, the Indian train bomb attacks, and last year's Indonesian earthquake. Lukwesa, who combines her career with housework and being a mother, would like to encourage more African women to become news presenters. "It is very important for African women, both white and black, to get involved in the media," she says. "Those stories can be given a voice and reflect who is in the world and what the world is about".

> *"New" and "developing" countries . . . recognise the advantages of enhancing their national profile in challenging the hitherto hegemony of* Miss World *and* Miss Universe.

Beauty Pageants as Springboard

Elsewhere, Rosemary Chileshe's career has provided a blueprint for what a beauty title and its holder should be. She was a student from Sheffield, a comparatively provincial "backwater"—though she has since moved to Manchester. Rosemary was voted Miss Zambia UK in 2003, then one of the several competing national community titles. Sheffield, however, is noted for its production of steel, and there has been steel in Rosemary's character. She has transformed her title and expectations of her compatriots.

In 2004, she returned home to compete for Zambia and qualified to represent her country in the *Miss World* pageant in China that same year. Rosemary has since gone on to use her celebrity status to strengthen and develop the embryonic pageant industry.

She has become a familiar guest at other promotions—always punctual (even though she has to travel from the other end of the UK to London), always well-groomed and beautiful, and always polite and modest.

She has become the epitome of what African beauty—and all beauty—should be. Unlike some other title-holders in the community, who seem to consider it to be their duty to discourage potential successors, she has stimulated newcomers to emulate her example.

In 2007, she represented Zambia again in the *Miss Universe* pageant in Mexico City. She showed Africans that they "could come good" at the highest level—and the floodgates were open. Yet Rosemary, who is a commercial property surveyor, has progressed considerably from her start in beauty pageants. It would require more space than is available to list her modelling achievements and her work as a goodwill ambassador in the fight against HIV/AIDS and poverty worldwide, in connection with which she addressed an international audience at a Commonwealth Forum to commemorate World AIDS Day 2006. Justina Mutale, who provided Rosemary's first platform for public recognition, has also developed from being just the promoter of *Miss Zambia UK*. As CEO of Perryfield Promotions, she now holds the franchise for 15 international beauty pageants around the world, including Miss Earth (Philippines), Miss Commonwealth (London), Miss Global International (Jamaica), World Miss University (South Korea), Miss Teen World (Ecuador and Australia), Miss Europe & World Junior (Czech Republic), Miss Teen Universe (Trinidad & Tobago) and the Face of the Universe (Ghana).

Pageants Promote Nations

Pageant "mania" seems to have broken out worldwide as the "new" and "developing" countries of Africa, Asia, Latin America and Eastern Europe recognise the advantages of enhancing their national profile in challenging the hitherto hegemony of *Miss World* and *Miss Universe*.

At the time of going to press, Justina was due to accompany, as chaperone, the 16 year-old Zambian beauty Anne Choolwe Malambo to the *Miss Europe & World Junior 2007* in Ostrava (Czech Republic).

Justina said: "In the past only the titleholder was given an opportunity to represent Zambia at an international pageant. However, with numerous international beauty pageants spread across the world, we want to spread our wings to all the four corners of the world by sending a candidate to fly the Zambian flag in each continent."

And for the title-holders it does not end when they have given up their title—as Emma Chishimba, an early *Miss Zambia UK*, went on to win *Miss Commonwealth Africa*.

Hildah Mulenga, chief executive of *Miss Malaika UK*, has shown that the UK Zambian community has room for two major promoters.

The pageant draws contestants from all the African Diaspora and, similarly, provides opportunities for others to compete for the most prestigious international titles. Earlier this year, Cynthia Muvirimi, a Zimbabwean midwife and First Princess Miss Malaika UK, won *Miss Global International* at the Pegasus Hotel in Kingston, Jamaica.

In doing so, she took over the crown from her compatriot Ropafadzai Garise in putting Zimbabwe in the spotlight and promoting Zimbabwean tourism. Cynthia was accompanied by Brenda Mulenga (Hildah's daughter) who, too, has "moved up" from being a contestant to helping with the administration and grooming the entrants.

Finding myself sitting at a recent press conference in London between Brenda Akot, Miss East Africa 2006, and Esta Lumutenga, Deputy Miss Caribbean & Commonwealth, I asked the former, somewhat naively, if all Ugandan women were so beautiful.

She replied: "All African women are beautiful". It is certainly impossible to argue with the evidence, and if Zambians are in the vanguard of the promotion and presentation of such high-profile activities, the other African communities are not far—if at all—behind.

11

Prohibiting Pageants in Muslim Countries Is Worse Than Allowing Them

Katha Pollitt

Katha Pollitt is a poet and critic. She is well known for her bi-weekly column "Subject to Debate" in The Nation *magazine.*

Religious fanaticism in the Muslim world led to a bloody protest in Nigeria against the Miss World pageant to be held there in 2002. Beauty pageants are not good for women since they disseminate false myths about beauty and parade women around like cattle. However, Islamic fundamentalism that prohibits beauty pageants and mandates that women keep covered by burkas (a garment that covers the entire body except for the eyes) is even worse for women.

The war between religious fanaticism and secular modernity is fought over women's bodies. Feminists have been saying this for years, not that anyone important was listening, but the Miss World riots [November 2002] in Kaduna, Nigeria, should make it obvious even to the dead white males at the *Washington Post*. Muslims, already on edge due to the presence in their country of so many lovelies on display, were apparently driven out of their minds by journalist Isioma Daniel's suggestion in the Lagos-based newspaper *ThisDay* that Mohammed "would probably have chosen a wife among them." By the time the smoke cleared and the bloody knives were put away, the local offices of the paper had been destroyed; more than 200 people, mostly Christian, had been murdered; hundreds more had been injured; and at least 4,500 left homeless. Nothing for the contestants to worry about, though: According to President Olusegun Obasanjo, "It could happen any time irresponsible journalism is committed against Islam." When in doubt, blame free speech. Nonetheless, the pageant relocated to London, while the governor of Zamfara State issued a *fatwa* [religious opinion on Islamic law] (later rescinded) against Ms. Daniel, urging Muslims to kill her—"Just like the blasphemous Indian writer Salman Rushdie, the blood of Isioma Daniel can be shed." She fled the country.

Say what you will about beauty pageants, if it's bikinis versus burkas, you've got to be for bathing suits.

Bikinis over Burkas

Not a good week for cultural relativism, on the whole.

Militant Islam may be the beginning of the end for multiculturalism, the live-and-let-live philosophy that asks, Why can't we all enjoy our differences? Ethnic food and world music are all very well, but *fatwas* and amputations and suicide bombings just don't put a smile on the day. In twelve Nigerian states, Sharia is now the law of the land, and in the background of the Miss Word fiasco lies the case of Amina Lawal, condemned to death by stoning by a Sharia court for the crime of having a baby out of wedlock. Because of the shocking brutality of the verdict and its blatant misogyny—needless to say, the man who impregnated her was not charged—some feminists had unsuccessfully urged the Miss World Pageant to boycott Nigeria, and a number of contestants—Misses Denmark, Panama, Costa Rica, Switzerland and South Africa—refused to take part. They are the true heroines of this discouraging episode.

Say what you will about beauty pageants, if it's bikinis versus burkas, you've got to be for bathing suits. British feminists who condemned the pageant as a sexist cattle call seemed to be missing the point, somehow. Yes, it's a sexist cattle call. And yes, the Miss World Pageant, seen each year by more than 2 billion viewers around the globe, helps disseminate white Western ideals of female beauty—and the concomitant body-image problems—to yet more distant lands (last year's winner, Miss Nigeria, the first black African winner, is, unlike most Nigerian women, *Vogue*-model slim). But that is not the big story right now. The big story is the growing power of fundamentalist maniacs.

Islamic feminists can surely find in the Koran proof of Allah's commitment to women's rights.

Speaking of whom, no one is getting more mileage out of Islamic fundamentalism than Christian fundamentalists. Many divines have been quick to portray Christianity as the religion of peace and love as opposed to the murderous, false teachings of Islam. Franklin Graham, Billy's son, who spoke at [former-U.S. president George W.] Bush's inauguration [in 2001], said Islam is "a very evil and wicked religion." Jerry Falwell has called Mohammed a "terrorist"—a "pedophile," too, chimed in the Rev. Jerry Vine. While President Bush keeps gamely asserting that Islam is a religion of peace, the foreign-policy hard right rolls its eyes. The Koran inherently leads to terrorism, [author] Norman Podhoretz argues, because it commands Muslims "to wage holy war, or jihad, against the 'infidels.'" Does that make the Gospels responsible for anti-Semitism? Not as long as right-wing Christians are Israel's best friends.

Muslim Feminists

And what do Muslim feminists, caught in the middle, make of all this? Given the bad image of Western feminism in the

Muslim world, it's not surprising that they make their way carefully. On a recent segment of *Democracy Now!* Fawzia Afzal-Khan and Azizah al-Hibri insisted passionately that the conviction of Amina Lawal was against Islamic law—where were the four male witnesses to the act of penetration? Why wasn't the man charged too? What about the doctrine of the sleeping fetus (don't ask)? The problem wasn't the Koran but its corruption, both agreed, going on to energetically bash Western feminists for obsessing about the veil instead of poverty and the United States for promoting Islamic extremists from Gen. Zia ul-Haq of Pakistan to bin Laden himself. "Islam," said al-Hibri, "gives women all the rights we are calling for." And yet, by the end of the program, Afzal-Khan was speaking sympathetically of separating mosque and state.

I'm no expert—to me the Koran, like the Old and New Testaments, seems both implicitly and explicitly sexist, and retrograde in other ways as well. Still, the human mind is a wonderful thing and modernity is a powerful force. We don't kill witches anymore, although Exodus explicitly bids us to, or cite the Bible to justify slavery, indentured servitude, polygymy, forcibly marrying widows to their brothers-in-law or impregnating the maid if the wife is infertile, after the example of Abraham. Even the humiliating Jewish menstrual laws have been reinterpreted under the pressure of feminism and the sexual revolution: Suddenly, after thousands of years, they're not about pollution and uncleanness, they're about giving women more power in the bedroom and having a more meaningful marriage. Moreover, they are retroactively understood to have always contained this meaning. Christian feminists have no trouble contextualizing out of existence even the most plainly worded of St. Paul's numerous male-supremacist commands: Women, obey your husbands, keep silent in church, cover your heads and all the rest. Religious texts mean what people want them to mean, and always have. If the whole elaborate institution of the papacy can be balanced on a single remark of Jesus to Peter (a remark that to Protestants, of course, means something quite different), Islamic feminists can surely find in the Koran proof of Allah's commitment to women's rights. It won't be a perfect fit, any more than modern feminist readings of the Bible are a perfect fit, but it will do for the time being.

12

Miss Landmine Beauty Pageant Helps Landmine Victims

Morten Traavik, as told to Robyn Stubbs

Morten Traavik is a Norwegian artist, actor, and director. He is also the founder of the Miss Landmine project.

The Miss Landmine project is a beauty pageant that is part art project and part humanitarian program. It is very different from an ordinary beauty pageant, since all participants are landmine victims who have been disabled in some way. Feminist critics and others who see the project as exploitative fail to understand that it actually subverts the stereotypes of traditional beauty pageants and proposes new ways of defining what it means to be beautiful. The women are chosen to participate for reasons other than having perfect looks—all they need is the willing desire to take part in the program.

The Miss Landmine project was born in my head about three and a half years ago, when I visited Angola for the first time. Landmines were a very tangible, almost physically oppressive feeling for me when I [was] there in 2003, because the very long civil war had just ended the year before. There were still very strong restrictions as to where one could move outside of the big cities because the whole countryside was, and is still, littered with landmines.

Morten Traavik, as told to Robyn Stubbs, "Redefining Beauty: Crowning Miss Landmine," *Orato*, November 28, 2007. Reproduced by permission.

A Different Kind of Beauty Pageant

Another strong but contrasting impression was attending a beauty pageant that the street kids in the back alley behind my ex-father-in-law's house had put together on New Year's Eve. It struck me as being so different from all the sleaze and the commercialism and the sexism that we, in our western culture, associate with those kinds of pageants.

On the contrary, it was a feel-good experience; it was more like a street party with all the neighborhood attending. The kids organized everything themselves, with girls from seven to 17 parading up and forth, and going through all the regular motions of a beauty contest with great earnestness and dedication.

It certainly has been my objective all along that Miss Landmine would have a political or humanitarian impact.

That being said, it wasn't really that serious—wasn't like the movie *Little Miss Sunshine* [2006]. It was a far cry from that; it was very inclusive and a much more heartwarming experience that was less based on physical perfection.

As a director and actor of theater and film to start with, willingly or unwillingly I have my sensibilities open to impressions that might result in some ideas for future projects. When I was approached by an art festival that was to take place in Angola's capital, Luanda, I quite quickly came up with the idea of trying to merge those two impressions.

Political Art Without Pity

Is it an art project? Is it a humanitarian project? Is it both? I would say that first and foremost, being an artist, I view it as an art project. But it certainly has been my objective all along that Miss Landmine would have a political or humanitarian impact.

What is special about Miss Landmine is exactly that: It is difficult to limit its definition to just one genre. Rather, it's more of a hybrid project which is on the borderline between artificiality and reality, and between arts and public service.

The main criterion is that the woman or girl wants to participate. To want to participate in a project like Miss Landmine and having been disabled by mines to an extent, it automatically follows that you are quite comfortable with the way you look and your own disability.

I have turned away some would-be participants for being too young, for instance. But I haven't turned away anybody for not being glamorous enough.

All the potential participants I have met personally about the project, and those I've heard have been approached by my Angolan organizers, have been very positive. The only reserved reactions have been 'Can this really be true?' They have to take some time to realize that this is a serious undertaking and a serious project.

For those women taking part, I really try to avoid speaking too much on their behalf. I can just speak about my impressions from working with them, and that is they all immensely enjoyed being allowed to have fun, and not being regarded as a victim or someone to be pitied or condescended. Rather, they were just like any other contemporary Angolan woman.

Controversy and Criticism

The criticism so far has been variations over the same theme, which is that beauty contests are the work of the devil and should be banished in any possible form or shape or color. For me, that is a kind of criticism people are entitled to have, but it doesn't really open up for any meaningful kind of discussion.

If you are not able to see that the beauty pageant in this particular situation is not an end in and of itself, but rather a means of expression to get a message across, I really don't know what to say. I am in danger of sounding a bit arrogant, but that criticism puts you on a level of perception that makes it very difficult to understand what Miss Landmine is really about.

If you look at this as an exploitative project, you are maybe a little bit stuck in the past.

There is a huge difference in the cultural perception of beauty pageants, but Miss Landmine can be interpreted in many ways. What surprises me a little bit is that the self-appointed feminist critics, who are deriding the project as sexist, don't appreciate Miss Landmine as a subversive project that is hollowing out the concept of beauty pageants from within. Among other things, it's also a very potent comment on exactly the sentiment that beauty pageants are superficial and solely focused on physical looks.

I have also been accused of exploiting these women, and from mostly the same people who are critical [of] beauty pageants. But I think if you look at this as an exploitative project, you are maybe a little bit stuck in the past.

Maybe that criticism was true in the colonial period, but we are actually past that now, and one of [the] things I am trying to achieve with the project is overcoming those stereotypes. Just because I'm white and male and come from a wealthy country, does that automatically make me an exploiter of presumably poor, black African women?

Assuming that this working relationship between Miss Landmine and the Angolan participants is one of exploitation is, I find, incredibly condescending towards the ladies themselves. You're assuming they don't know what's good for them.

It's also a paid assignment. Both the photo session and the participation in the live pageant itself are paid assignments, so it's also a job that they are doing to promote their own situation and awareness of landmine and disability issues.

What do I see when I look at the pictures of Miss Landmine contestants? In danger of sounding a bit overblown and Hollywood-like, I think I see true beauty. I see beautiful women who are proud, dignified and comfortable with who they are. They radiate a strong joy of being encouraged to be sexy and funky and attractive and glamorous.

And that strong, feel-good factor is all the while undermined by the tragic and quite horrible back-stories of mutilation and war that [inevitably] stays with a landmine survivor. It is a picture of ambiguity, but where the forces of life prevail.

13

Miss Landmine
Beauty Pageant Exploits
Landmine Victims

Expat Advisory Services (EAS)

Expat Advisory Services is a Web site offering news, opinion, and advice targeted at expatriates living in Cambodia, South Korea, Thailand, Laos, and Vietnam.

The second Miss Landmine beauty pageant, to be held in Cambodia in 2009, should be banned. The first Miss Landmine beauty pageant, held in Angola in 2008, prompted many valid feminist arguments in opposition to it. Cambodian women who are the victims of landmines are at risk for being exploited by the pageant. These women would be much better served by using the pageant money to help them in more practical ways, which does not include uprooting them from their remote villages to compete in an exploitative beauty contest.

Take 24 pretty but mainly poor and under-educated female amputee landmine victims from the provinces, get a bunch of foreigners to dress them up, and make them compete in a beauty pageant in which the main prize is prosthetic limbs.

Does that sound acceptable? According to the overwhelmingly male voices backing the project, Miss Landmine Cambodia 2009 is "for their own good."

The Cambodian Mine Action Authority's chief Sam Sotha, who is also a member of the prime minister's cabinet, is so

Expat Advisory Services (EAS), "Miss Landmine Cambodia—'For Their Own Good,'" April 23, 2008. Reproduced by permission.

impressed he signed a letter of support for the project despite the government's September 2006 ban on beauty contests of any kind.

Feminist Concerns About Angola's Pageant

The competition is the brainchild of Norwegian theatre director and artist Morten Traavik, who says people who object to amputee women in bikinis and on runways are closed minded and underestimate the women involved.

Other prizes include household appliances (wonderful for the little ladies who are lucky enough to have electricity in their village) and modeling shoots which will feature in a glossy Miss Landmine Magazine—one it is doubtful many of the contestants can read or even afford.

Miss Landmine Angola 2008, held this month [April 2008], was a huge hit, Mr Traavik says, and the overwhelming disgust over the project voiced by African feminists in blogs and articles was unwarranted. Mr Traavik, however, does little to reassure on his own attitudes to women.

Of feminist Sokari Ekine, who has written for on-line journals and websites in both Africa and Norway, he wrote "Respected feminist? Give me a break. She is just a blogger, and a pretty stupid one at that."

But do these women have a point? When Sokari Ekine's website Black Looks condemned the African pageant, there seemed to be some very valid points put on the table by other bloggers.

"These middleclass/rich Norwegian folks would be better received petitioning the western companies and governments that produce and allow the distribution of these offensive weapons," wrote Obi.

"As a trans man I am all too familiar with this kind of apparent fetishizing of difference. File this one under 'Wrong. Very wrong' then spread the word," added Jay Sennet.

"This is really disgusting. Particularly sinister is the white people primping the women. . . . Provocative for the sake of it rather than serving any useful or empowering purpose," wrote Heidi of pictures on the Miss Landmine website showing contestants being prepared.

And Hippo asked whether spending the US$80,000 it cost to put on the pageant might not have been better spent giving them an education or teaching them a skill.

"(Then) they could escape the discrimination they have to live with by demonstrating the useful contribution to society that they could make. Seeing them as productive citizens would do more to highlight the inhuman horror of landmines."

The pageant . . . opens them up to the possibility of exploitation, including sexual exploitation.

Exploitation of Cambodian Women

Cambodian contestants will face similar challenges. Will a few nights in a nice hotel they will never be able to visit again and a gift of the gowns they wear on the night (donated by a label they can never afford) help these girls back in their province?

How useful is an evening gown and a designer bikini to an amputee mother on a rice farm in Kampot?

Whether Mr Traavik likes it or not, the pageant also opens them up to the possibility of exploitation, including sexual exploitation—if beauty pageants are not exploitative enough, whether they be able bodied or not.

Bringing vulnerable girls from remote areas to the city for a one-night cattle parade before the project leaves Cambodia, possibly never to return, opens the women up to all sorts of new dangers.

The main problem Miss Landmine faces is sustainability—it just isn't sustainable, and that is why it has raised suspicions it is exploitative. How is this project different from a foreigner walking in to a girlie bar, giving a sex worker money for a one night stand and then saying he has helped her regain her self esteem?

What's next in Mr Traavik's humanitarian drive? Miss Genocide, where the winner is granted a stay of execution? Miss HIV/AIDS, where the winner receives a year's supply of anti-retrovirals? Miss Human Rights Abuses, where the winner is not beaten?

Why hasn't Mr Traavik seen fit to hold this pageant in a developed country? Why is he choosing the most vulnerable women from one of the most vulnerable social groups in some of the poorest parts of the world?

It's disappointing the Cambodian men who have approved this "freak show," as Mr Traavik himself has jokingly referred to it, have apparently not considered these issues.

Hopefully the government will uphold its ban on beauty parades and, if Mr Traavik really cares, he will put the money to good use in Cambodia anyway without having to stage his heavily sponsored and potentially lucrative show, or taking his modeling shots to fill his expensive magazine and then dumping these women right back where they started while he gets on a plane.

14

Child Beauty Pageants Reflect the Culture's Sexualization of Children

James R. Kincaid

James R. Kincaid is the Aerol Arnold Professor of English at the University of Southern California and the author of Erotic Innocence: The Culture of Child Molesting.

Our culture's obsession with the murder of child beauty pageant participant JonBenet Ramsey reflects a sick fixation on the eroticization of children. People who voyeuristically indulge in stories like JonBenet's, and the media's reporting of them, reflect a broader disease in our society, one that treats children as both innocent victims and erotic spectacles. Beauty-pageant parents are often unfairly charged with being the problem when, in fact, all parents subject their children to behaviors similar to the activities of child beauty pageants. Until the culture as a whole confronts this obsession, such eroticization of children will continue within child beauty pageants and elsewhere.

It probably shouldn't surprise us that JonBenet, like Roderick Usher's sister [from the short story "The Fall of the House of Usher" by Edgar Allan Poe], won't stay buried. It's the return of the repressed all over again, here before us, strutting its stuff and doing its cultural work because we so badly need it. Where else can we find forbidden material served up to us in ways we can both enjoy and disown? We

James R. Kincaid, "Little Miss Sunshine: America's Obsession with JonBenet Ramsey," *Slate*, August 21, 2006. Reprinted with permission.

have to deal with a most uncomfortable heritage: an "innocent" child who is also deeply eroticized. That's an unthinkable idea, but JonBenet is one of those stories that allows us to think it.

A Cultural Obsession

It's not just the JonBenet affair that does this return act for us: We had Michael Jackson in two distinct performances, also separated by a decade, and pedophile Catholic priests in a reprise as well. Even McMartin [preschool abuse trials in the 1980s and 1990s] came as a double-header drama. When things are running a little low in the erotic-child-spectacle area, we simply reach into the well and draw up again what has served us so richly in the past.

JonBenet takes to the runway again because a happy confluence of events gives us the chance to put her there. It's really all our doing, even if the police helped out. True, we have a confession of sorts from one John Mark Karr, but the criminal case seems to be melting before our eyes as the days pass. CNN lets us know that the confession will keep us busy for some time: "Far from laying to rest the 10-year mystery of who killed JonBenet Ramsey, the stunning admission . . . only deepened speculation about whether the soft-spoken schoolteacher committed the crime."

The discourse is alive; the game is afoot. Makes one wonder if we aren't giving Karr's background and confession so much prominence because they feed our deep personal needs and not the needs of justice. Just why is it we need to hear, once again, about JonBenet and the beauty pageants, the murder and the bad parents, about the little body unveiled?

We know about Karr, it turns out, largely because he carried on a four-year correspondence with a University of Colorado journalism professor, Michael Tracey, who finally became "concerned" this past May [2006] and took the e-mails to authorities, who moved with some speed to make the arrest.

Tracey, the producer of three documentaries on the JonBenet case, is motivated, he says, by the desire to show how overblown the coverage is: "I don't regard JonBenet's murder as an important story." He is publicizing it to demonstrate its insignificance and to illustrate what is wrong with American journalism.

Now, there's a dedicated ironist for you: He spends all this time illustrating what a trivial subject he has! But, of course, Tracey badly misses the point: JonBenet would not get all this attention did we not want to bestow it. It's not the media forcing on us something we'd rather not have: We're lining up at the trough to be fed. The story has too much in it for us, even if the murder part of it is, as Tracey suspects, window dressing.

The Real Problem

This story allows us to fulminate against trivial problems while ignoring huge problems close to home, meanwhile wallowing in self-righteous porn babble: We are able to use the half-clothed bodies of children as centerfolds while professing shock that anyone would so display them. The story is always the same: Somebody else finds the bodies of children irresistible and we want the chance to rail against these monsters, meanwhile relishing the details of the very bodies we claim indifference to. It is a classic example of scapegoating.

For kids really do not fare very well in our culture: Millions of children are, in fact, abused in unspeakable ways. Five hundred thousand kids every year are classified as "throwaways" (children whose parents or guardians will not let them live at home, as distinguished from "runaways"). As many as 800,000 are beaten horribly. Even more are subject to emotional abuse and neglect. How much attention do they get? Instead, we focus our attention, almost all of it, on stranger-danger: things like abductions, of which there are between 100 and 200 annually. Our carefully controlled outrage is generated for our own purposes, certainly not to protect the children.

Whining at beauty contest parents generally is a favorite pastime of ours, as if such pageants were freakish, rather than a version of a central parenting activity: parading kids, sexualizing them, putting them on display.

And when kids are indeed abused, who is doing it? Mom and Dad and Uncle Ted and Aunt May. As little as 2 percent of child abuse is committed by strangers. Again, why are we exercised over JonBenet?

Manufacturing Good and Bad Parents

The case does many things for us, of course. It makes us feel both titillated and virtuous; it makes us feel smart. Most centrally, it makes flattering distinctions between good parents (us) and bad parents (the Ramseys). Even if the Ramseys didn't kill their daughter, they exposed her to lascivious eyes in beauty contests, which is about as bad. Notice how much press is directed to abusing the Ramseys, to suggesting that (unlike us) their relationship to their child was unhealthy, vicious, exploitative. This whining at beauty contest parents generally is a favorite pastime of ours, as if such pageants were freakish, rather than a version of a central parenting activity: parading kids, sexualizing them, putting them on display.

The current film *Little Miss Sunshine* is a good example of how much we need to separate healthy families (ours) from diseased ones (those who sexualize kids). That film goes so far in its eagerness to pander to audiences as to imagine domestic bliss as the ability to be repulsed by and unite against sexy kids (beauty queens). Such hypocrisy plays to the uneasiness of audiences who, in real life, would find the lumpy little heroine of the film utterly disgusting, turning from her to feast their eyes on little vamps.

The Ramseys frighten us by being so much like the parents in the film—and like the audience: voyeurs gazing at their own children. Looking at kids is arguably our culture's central activity, so long as we can successfully objectify the kids, make them strangely doll-like and immune, both fetching and innocent. We want the Ramseys to be like the parents of Polly Klaas [murdered in 1993], or other tragic figures who occupy the center of such dramas. *What could be more horrifying for parents than to lose a child to a stranger?* Even when the child is not killed, we are fond of saying that rape is somehow "worse" than murder. Worse for whom? For the parent, of course, whose rights have been violated and whose part in this sick cultural drama has been stolen.

Our Cultural Subconscious

Several of the recent crime-news commentators, struggling to define JonBenet's charm without wading into treacherous waters, have compared her to Shirley Temple in her essential cuteness. Big mistake. [Author] Graham Greene decades ago was chased out of England for daring to analyze the ingredients of that Shirley Temple "cute" appeal. Greene said she was able to elicit excited "gasps" from "her antique audience" by twitching her "well-developed little rump" and generally exercising a "sidelong searching coquetry" "with the mature suggestiveness of a Dietrich."

Greene specified the lingering fantasy that JonBenet also plays out, one deep and dangerous in our cultural subconscious. We need to face down that fantasy and not pretend we can exorcise it on the likes of John Mark Karr or the supposed ills of American journalism. The fault lies not in such things but in us. JonBenet will not rest until our need for her finds an outlet less necrophilic.

15

Child Beauty Pageants Should Be Eliminated

Billy Reed

Billy Reed is a Kentucky-based newspaper columnist, magazine writer, radio talk-show host and guest, TV commentator, political pundit, and book author.

Child beauty pageants are a form of child abuse, since they exploit children and place them in harm's way. The children who participate in beauty pageants are often hurt by the experience, suffering damage to their self-esteem and later developing eating disorders, like anorexia, due to skewed values about their bodies. Additionally, dressing children up with adult clothes and makeup appeals to sexual predators, placing them at risk of falling victim to a pedophile. Because of these potential dangers to children, no one under the age of eighteen should be allowed to participate in beauty pageants.

Looking through the lineup of events for the Kentucky State Fair, I noted the usual competitions for rooster-crowing, hog-calling, pie-baking, and watermelon-growing. Mercifully, the list did not include a corndog-eating contest. You know what I mean if you saw ESPN's coverage of the Nathan's Famous Hot-Dog Eating Contest at Coney Island in New York.

Child Pageants Are Child Abuse

But what made me happiest was that the State Fair doesn't sponsor a child beauty pageant. I thought those things were

Billy Reed, "Time to End Child Beauty Pageants," *Billy Reed Says*, August 28, 2006. Reproduced by permission.

sick long before the JonBenet Ramsey case. Now I know they are. In fact, I would support a movement to make beauty pageants illegal for anybody under the age of 18.

Until the JonBenet case resurfaced last week [August 19, 2006], I hadn't thought about it since the day last winter when *The Courier-Journal* ran a startling photo on the front page of the Metro section.

Some parents are so warped, so starved for attention or some kind of self-validation, that they will shamelessly exploit their children's physical beauty without regard for the possible consequences.

It was taken at either a child beauty pageant or a cheer-leading competition. It showed several girls under the age of 10, their sweet young faces tarted up with makeup and their hair fixed in adult fashions. My first thought was, "Every pedophile who sees this will cut it out and paste it on his wall."

Understand, I wasn't blaming the newspaper. If anything, it was doing the public a service by reminding us that some parents are so warped, so starved for attention or some kind of self-validation, that they will shamelessly exploit their children's physical beauty without regard for the possible consequences.

When I mentioned my utter contempt for child beauty pageants to my college friend Stephanie McGann, a mother and retired teacher in Fayette County, she immediately snapped, "It's child abuse."

And it is, by official definition.

According to the Child Abuse Prevention and Treatment and Adoption Reform Act, child abuse is "the physical or mental injury, sexual abuse or exploitation, of a child under circumstances which indicate the child's health or welfare is threatened or harmed."

Exposing Children to Danger

The danger from sexual predators is only part of the problem. Defenders of child beauty pageants argue that they teach self-confidence and poise. But studies have shown that for every child who may derive some benefit from the competition, hundreds of others suffer damage to their self-esteem and develop warped values about their bodies, which often lead to anorexia or bulimia.

Due to the ever-increasing proliferation of cable TV and the internet, child abuse is an even bigger problem today than it was almost a decade ago, when JonBenet was found murdered in the basement of her home in Colorado Springs.

Over and again, the Fox News Network and its ilk showed photos and videotape of JonBenet competing in beauty pageants. Here she was dancing, singing, smiling, flirting. Shirley Temple redux. But where Shirley at least was allowed to be a little girl, JonBenet was made up, coiffed, and dressed to look far older than her age, which was six at the time.

[The parents of JonBenet Ramsey] put their child in harm's way by exploiting her publicly in child beauty pageants.

Six! Most girls her age were still playing with dolls. Instead, JonBenet *was* a doll—a living, breathing Barbie—with which her parents were playing. It didn't take a psychologist to figure out that her mother, Patsy, herself a former beauty queen, was reliving her unfulfilled fantasties through her daughter.

It was just . . . so . . . tacky! And disgusting. And dangerous. And perfect for the 24-hour cable TV channels that rose to prominence during the O.J. Simpson murder trial and were hungry for the next sordid sex story.

When I heard that authorities had arrested a suspect in Thailand and that he had confessed to the murder, I knew what was coming. Sure enough, it was virtually impossible to click on a cable news network last weekend [August 19–20, 2006] without encountering a Greta Van Sustern or a Larry King interviewing some "expert" or about the case. And like a recurring nightmare, here was all the old JonBenet footage, just as disturbing now as it was then. Most of the speculation centered around whether the suspect's confession was real or whether he was just another sicko looking for his 15 minutes of fame. But whether he's the killer or not, I don't think it lets JonBenet's parents, particularly her mother, who died recently of cancer, off the hook. They put their child in harm's way by exploiting her publicly in child beauty pageants. The suspect said that's how he became aware of her and interested in her—an admission that should give pause to every parent who's even considering putting their child into a beauty pageant. Thank heavens there's no such animal at the State Fair.

16

Teen Beauty Pageants Can Teach Teens Many Valuable Life Lessons

Jennifer Trujillo

Jennifer Trujillo is a former beauty pageant contestant who is associate professor in the teacher education department at Fort Lewis College, Durango, Colorado.

Beauty pageants can teach teens many valuable lessons. Learning to be articulate, to be confident, and developing a thick skin are all important traits that can serve one well beyond the pageant world. Though there are legitimate feminist concerns about beauty pageants, there are also positive benefits to participating in the contests. The views about pageants, both for and against, need to be balanced to get an accurate perspective about teenage participation in these events.

"How much do you want for these?" The silver haired lady asked me. She held up two rhinestone crowns that glinted in the sunlight. It was 1992, and I was selling some of my old things at a rummage sale to raise money the summer before I finished college. I took my chances. "Ten dollars apiece," I replied. As the woman fished the money out of her purse, she paused and said, "Honey, are you sure you want to sell these? You might have a little girl someday who would love to play with them." I responded emphatically that no daughter of mine would ever have any use for them. I had won these crowns, along with others, in beauty pageants years ago.

Benefits of Participating in a Pageant

The evolution of my femininity is complicated. When I began entering pageants in my teens, I was trying to showcase my talents and earn money for college. I was a vocalist and thought of pageants as singing contests. Plus, my mother was Venezuelan, and I spent years of my childhood in the beauty-saturated culture of Caracas. Venezuela is known for amassing great numbers of Miss Universe titles—why shouldn't I aspire to join the ranks? After all, it was in my blood.

I was a relative latecomer to pageant "systems" and soon found I had a lot to learn. These systems were worlds of their own. They were rife with political and economic undercurrents. Other girls had coaches and thousands of dollars for gowns; I had neither. Still, I capitalized on the good will of others, got sponsors and moved forward. Pageant judges looked for beauty and poise, as well as an impressive interview. While some girls made a mockery of any one of the three, I was determined to succeed. I started as a naive and apathetic teen and transformed myself into someone who articulated informed opinions about current events.

> *I started as a naive and apathetic teen and transformed myself into someone who articulated informed opinions about current events.*

I learned how to speak in a formal interview, walk with grace and project confidence. I met some girls who were so cutthroat in their pursuit of crowns that they'd eat you alive just to taste the rhinestones. I found false smiles and fake enthusiasm. I encountered insecurity and girls who'd been doing this since the age of 3, following a path set forth by their mothers. Behind the smiles, I found some true unhappiness manifesting itself in destructive behavior, including eating disorders. I myself once dieted on oranges and water for so many weeks that the inside of my mouth was filled with canker sores. All my friends told me I looked great, and we loved the misery of dieting.

Despite all that, I found camaraderie and made some genuine friends. There were late nights full of giggles and shared anxiety. We bonded through the varying verbal attacks or adoration of the crowd. I developed a thick skin and reeled off a quick response when I was asked on a radio show how I could "parade myself around like a piece of meat." I was a staunch supporter of pageants and I defended myself at every turn. After all, I was saving money for my education.

When I graduated and joined the real world, it was both my college education and the skills I'd acquired in pageants that helped me become successful.

Balancing the Views Toward Pageants

Then I got to college and my world went topsy-turvy. I was hearing all sorts of new ideas, and I began to second-guess myself and my motives. In political-science and sociology courses, I saw the error of my ways. How could I have demeaned myself and my entire gender? I became a feminist and was ashamed of my past. The truth of the matter included the fact that some of my pageant earnings paid a portion of my college tuition.

In the end, I found a way to balance both perspectives. When I graduated and joined the real world, it was both my college education and the skills I'd acquired in pageants that helped me become successful. I had interview experience. I knew how to handle people who were fake, ambitious and out to win. I could deflect negativity and work as part of a team. I loved people and learning about new things. I continued my educational pursuits and eventually earned a doctoral degree. I still list "Miss America Scholar" on my résumé and wonder if it will draw snickers in my academic world. But like any life lesson, I see both the positive and negative aspects of the experience. Looking back, I feel no disdain. The experience taught me a lot.

Today, like so many other women, I balance a career and motherhood. I think back to what that lady said at the rummage sale. She was right. I now have two little girls who love to play dress-up, and I wish I had not sold those crowns. They are a part of my past and they symbolize who I became.

Organizations to Contact

The editors have compiled the following list of organizations concerned with the issues debated in this book. The descriptions are derived from materials provided by the organizations. All have publications or information available for interested readers. The list was compiled on the date of publication of the present volume; the information provided here may change. Be aware that many organizations take several weeks or longer to respond to inquiries, so allow as much time as possible.

A Minor Consideration
15003 S. Denker Ave., Gardena, CA   90247
fax: (310) 523-3691
Web site: www.minorcon.org

A Minor Consideration is a nonprofit foundation formed to give guidance and support to child performers, including child beauty pageant participants. The foundation works to provide a strong emphasis on education and character development, plus helps to preserve the money these children generate. The foundation offers many articles on its Web site, including original editorials on the topic of child performers.

Child Welfare Information Gateway
1250 Maryland Ave. SW, Eighth Fl., Washington, DC   20024
(800) 394-3366
e-mail: info@childwelfare.gov
Web site: www.childwelfare.gov

Child Welfare Information Gateway is a service of the Children's Bureau in the Administration for Children and Families, part of the U.S. Department of Health and Human Services. The agency promotes the safety, permanency, and well-being of children and families. Resources available at the Web site include definitions of child abuse and neglect, as well as risk factors for abuse.

Concerned Women for America (CWA)

1015 Fifteenth St. NW, Suite 1100, Washington, DC   20005

(202) 488-7000 • fax: (202) 488-0806

Web site: www.cwfa.org

Concerned Women for America is a public policy women's organization that has the goal of bringing Biblical principles into all levels of public policy. The Beverly LaHaye Institute of the CWA focuses on family issues, feminist and women's issues, and social and cultural concerns. Among the organization's brochures, fact sheets, and articles available on its Web site is "Miss America: The Rest of the Story."

Feminist Majority Foundation (FMF)

1600 Wilson Blvd., Suite 801, Arlington, VA   22209

(703) 522-2214 • fax: (703) 522-2219

Web site: www.feminist.org

The Feminist Majority Foundation, which was founded in 1987, is an organization dedicated to women's equality, reproductive health, and nonviolence. FMF engages in research and public policy development, public education programs, grassroots organizing projects, leadership training and development programs, and participates in and organizes forums on issues of women's equality and empowerment. A variety of literature is available on their Web site, as well as links to other resources such as feminist magazines.

Miss America Organization

222 New Rd., Suite 700, Linwood, NJ   08221

(609) 653-8700 • fax: (609) 653-8740

e-mail: info@missamerica.org

Web site: www.missamerica.org

The Miss America Organization runs the Miss America program. The Miss America program exists to provide personal and professional opportunities for young women to promote their voices in culture, politics, and the community. Available on its Web site is information about the competition, including key facts and figures about the history of the Miss America pageant, first held in 1921.

Miss Landmine Organization
e-mail: morten@miss-landmine.org
Web site: www.miss-landmine.org

The Miss Landmine Organization puts on beauty pageants for landmine victims, including the first Miss Landmine beauty pageant held in Angola in 2008 and the 2009 pageant in Cambodia. The organization aims to enhance female pride and empowerment, raise awareness about landmines, and question established concepts of physical beauty. The organization's Web site contains information, including links to news and commentary, about the pageants.

Miss Universe Organization
1370 Avenue of the Americas, 16th Fl., New York, NY   10019
(212) 373-4999 • fax: (212) 843-9200
e-mail: MissUPR@missuniverse.com
Web site: www.missuniverse.org

The Miss Universe Organization operates the Miss Teen USA, Miss USA, and Miss Universe pageants. The Miss USA beauty pageant, which has existed for over fifty years, aims to redefine the world's views of the women who attain its exclusive titles and communicate women's views of their own roles. Available on the Miss Universe Organization Web site is information about the organization and the three pageants.

National Organization for Women (NOW)
1100 H St. NW, 3rd Fl., Washington, DC   20005
(202) 628-8NOW • fax: (202) 785-8576
Web site: www.now.org

The National Organization for Women is a nonprofit organization devoted to furthering women's rights through education and litigation. For over a decade, NOW has led the Love

Your Body campaign, which has the goal of countering the unrealistic beauty standards, gender stereotypes, and sometimes harmful images imposed by media and advertisers on women. Available at NOW's Web site is information on the Love Your Body campaign, including information on staging a "mock beauty pageant."

Bibliography

Books

Maxine Leeds Craig	*Ain't I a Beauty Queen? Black Women, Beauty, and the Politics of Race.* New York: Oxford University Press, 2002.
Susan Dewey	*Making Miss India Miss World: Constructing Gender, Power, and the Nation in Postliberalization India.* Syracuse, NY: Syracuse University Press, 2008.
Brenda Foley	*Undressed for Success: Beauty Contestants and Exotic Dancers as Merchants of Morality.* New York: Palgrave Macmillan, 2005.
Henry A. Giroux	*Stealing Innocence: Corporate Culture's War on Children.* New York: Palgrave Macmillan, 2001.
Shari Graydon	*In Your Face: The Culture of Beauty and You.* Toronto, Ontario: Annick Press, 2004.
Sheila Jeffreys	*Beauty and Misogyny: Harmful Cultural Practices in the West.* New York: Psychology Press, 2005.
Rebecca Chiyoko King-O'Riain	*Pure Beauty: Judging Race in Japanese American Beauty Pageants.* Minneapolis: University of Minnesota Press, 2006.

Wendy McElroy — *Liberty for Women: Freedom and Feminism in the Twenty-first Century*. Chicago: Ivan R. Dee, 2002.

Elissa Stein — *Beauty Queen: Here She Comes*. San Francisco: Chronicle Books, 2006.

Elwood D. Watson and Darcy Martin, eds. — *"There She Is, Miss America": The Politics of Sex, Beauty, and Race in America's Most Famous Pageant*. New York: Palgrave Macmillan, 2004.

Naomi Wolf — *The Beauty Myth: How Images of Beauty Are Used Against Women*. New York: Harper Perennial, 2002.

Christine Reiko Yano — *Crowning the Nice Girl: Gender, Ethnicity, and Culture in Hawaii's Cherry Blossom Festival*. Honolulu: University of Hawaii Press, 2006.

Periodicals

Tom Bartlett — "Babeland! A Skeptical Father Ventures Deep Inside the World of Child Beauty Pageants—and Never Makes It Out," *Washington Post*, July 22, 2007.

David Beaver — "The Furor over Ms. Wheelchair America," *Palaestra*, Spring 2005.

Patty Bond — "Plumage and Pageantry," *WWD*, August 6, 2003.

Irin Carmon   "There She Is: Inside the Year of the
                           Harvard Beauty Queen," *The
                           Crimson*, September 25, 2003.
                           www.thecrimson.com.

Rachel Cooke   "Girls, Girls, Girls: Beauty Contests,
                           Once the Epitome of Glamour, Have
                           Been Driven Out by Feminism and
                           the Tabloids. But the Fake Tans,
                           Smiles, and Swimsuits Seem Almost
                           Innocent in Today's World of Botox,
                           Breast Implants, and Trout Pouts,"
                           New Statesman, June 14, 2004.

Denver Post   "Let Beauty Pageants Fade," June 28,
                           2007.

Akua Djannie   "Beauty Pageants—What Do They
                           Really Achieve?" *Africa News Service*,
                           May 15, 2007.

Owen Edwards   "American Idol: Once upon a Time,
                           Miss America Reigned Supreme,"
                           Smithsonian, January 2006.

Kaye Gibbons   "A Winning Life," *Real Simple*,
                           September 2006.

Olivia Gordon   "Backstage at Miss England," *Real*,
                           October 14, 2005.

Abigail Haworth   "Where Thin Isn't In," *Marie Claire*,
                           September 2003.

Boris Johnson   "Magnificently Sexist," *Spectator*,
                           September 24, 2005.

Jessica Kowal   "Lacking Big-City Luster, Junior Miss Carves a Niche," *New York Times*, April 2, 2007.

Dinah Kpodo   "The Explosion of Beauty Pageants," *Africa News Service*, September 4, 2006.

Jennifer B. Lee   "The Tiara Was Nice. Now Where's the Scholarship?" *New York Times*, September 24, 2007.

Ian MacKinnon   "Miss Landmine: Exploitation or Bold Publicity for the Victims?" *Guardian*, April 22, 2008.

Marie Claire   "Miss Landmine: The Beauty Pageant with a Difference," May 28, 2008.

Cahal Milmo   "Muslim Women Brave Wrath of Fundamentalist Competing in Miss England Beauty Contest," *Independent*, September 3, 2005.

Jina Moore   "From Noses to Hips, Rwandans Start to Redefine Beauty," *Christian Science Monitor*, July 18, 2008.

Elizabeth Nesoff   "In Search of Feminists," *Christian Science Monitor*, August 26, 2003.

Erika Orban   "Miss Landmine," asWoman.net, May 8, 2008. www.aswoman.net.

Iver Peterson   "'Fear Factor' Era Poses a Challenge for Miss America," *New York Times*, April 9, 2005.

Carla Power — "More than a Pretty Face," *Marie Claire*, June 2006.

Paulo Prada — "Felons All, but Free to Try Being Beauty Queen for a Day," *New York Times*, December 1, 2005.

Anna Quindlen — "There She Was. There She Goes," *Newsweek*, April 17, 2006.

Simon Robinson — "A Pageant with a Purpose," *Time International*, March 7, 2005.

Jim Yardley — "Beauty Contestant Fights for Right of Self-Improvement," *New York Times*, June 17, 2004, p. A4.

Emily Yoffe — "There She Is, Mrs. America...," *Slate*, July 8, 2004. www.slate.com.

Eileen Zurbriggen — "Message and the Media," February 26, 2007.

Index

Beauty pageants.

DATE			